CW00543377

To Rosnah

Best Wishes

[illegible]

29/1/05

JOEY YAP

Stories and Lessons on Feng Shui

玄明郎

風水

Stories and Lessons on Feng Shui

First Edition Oct 2004

The author can be reached at:

Mastery Academy of Chinese Metaphysics Sdn. Bhd.
19-3, The Boulevard, Mid Valley City,
Lingkaran Syed Putra,
59200 Kuala Lumpur, Malaysia.
Tel: +603-2284 8080, +603-2284 8318
Fax: +603-2284 1218
Email: info@masteryacademy.com
Website: www.masteryacademy.com

Published by JY Books Sdn. Bhd. (659134-T)

Artwork by Cynthia Tan Seen Ti
Thien Dimensions Sdn. Bhd. (550414-H)
www.thien-dimensions.com

INDEX OF STORIES

PREFACE

Feng Shui has become a subject of great interest in the last few years - just visit a bookshop and you'll see the bookshelves groaning under the weight of numerous books of all sizes and colours on the subject. The study of Feng Shui has today become a 'cottage industry'.

Quick fixes - watered down instant noodle versions of the real thing - have become popular in Feng Shui these days. It greatly concerns me that a respectable ancient science like Feng Shui is becoming more and more superficial, with even well-educated people finding it difficult to muster up any respect for Feng Shui.

Who could blame them when they are told that their life can change overnight if they just put an object in a certain corner of their room! In my consulting work, I have lost track of the number of times when I tell people I am a 'Feng Shui' consultant and the first thing they give me is a 'look' that says " You're now going to tell me about what I must buy to put around my house."

Many of my practicing students also suffer the same 'misunderstanding' and it normally takes hours in each meeting to explain to clients that there's nothing wrong with their decor and we are not in the business of 'interior decorations'. We are Classical Feng Shui practitioners.

This somewhat 'low' perception of Feng Shui is something which I hope to change. I wish to tell the world that there's really so much more to what 'really' is Feng Shui. And that it is really not just about quick fixes. It's a respectable science. Nothing to do with superstitions or old wives tales.

And that is what this book is all about.

I wanted to write something that would help people understand Feng Shui better and also let them know that what is generally known as Feng Shui today is not quite the same as what our past revered masters would regard as Classical Feng Shui. I wanted to introduce, in the form of short stories, the nuances, the essence, the concepts and the original ideas that were once part of what was 'traditionally' practiced as Feng Shui.

Another motivation behind this book is also the realisation that people are beginning to ask more serious questions about Feng Shui. They have begun to realize "wait a minute, it really CANNOT be as easy as putting something in the South West corner". And they are starting to ask more questions about the true principles and the true theories behind this classical field of Chinese Metaphysics. They are seeking guidance and simply wish to have some simple questions answered.

This is a special collection of essays and stories and the book has been designed so that you can always jump from chapter to chapter or browse the stories according to what takes your interest or fancy. There is no need to read it through from Chapter 1 till the end. I have however arranged the topics so that the simpler or easier to digest stories are at the start and the more technical and complicated ones are towards the back.

One of my favourite sections is the Mail Bag section, where I have included a selection of the many questions I have received over the years via e-mail from individuals all over the world, on all kinds of subjects related to Feng Shui.

I hope, after reading this collection of stories, you will gain a better understanding of what Classical Feng Shui is really all about as some of the well-known myths are debunked and the superstitions and taboos are explained away.

I have included stories on BaZi or Four Pillars of Destiny as well because BaZi is an essential complementary field of study to Feng Shui. BaZi, which is a form of Chinese Astrology, is very helpful in providing a broader perspective of Chinese Metaphysics. I hope that the stories I have selected will help you understand a little bit more about BaZi and how it complements Feng Shui.

I wish you the best in your endeavors and study of Feng Shui. Don't forget to check in to my website : www.masteryacademy.com for my latest articles, tools and multimedia downloads.

Joey Yap
August 31, 2004

MASTERY ACADEMY
OF CHINESE METAPHYSICS™

At www.masteryacademy.com, you will find some useful tools to ascertain key information about the Feng Shui of a property or for study of Astrology.

The Joey Yap Flying Star Calculator can be utilized to plot your home or office Flying Star chart. To find out your personal best directions, use the 8 Mansions Calculator. To learn more about your personal Destiny, you can use the Joey Yap BaZi Ming Pan Calculator to plot your Four Pillars of Destiny – you just need to have your date of birth (day, month, year) and time of birth.

For more information about BaZi, Xuan Kong or Flying Star Feng Shui, or if you wish to learn more about these subjects with Joey Yap, logon to the Mastery Academy of Chinese Metaphysics website at **www.masteryacademy.com**

Feng Shui: Back to the Future

It is important to always begin on the right footing in any study. In this first article, I would like to correct (and debunk) certain ideas about Feng Shui that have built up over the years. The idea here is to answer the WHEN, WHY and WHAT questions relating to Feng Shui.

Let's start with the origins of Feng Shui.

Many books, articles and websites offer different dates as to the origin of Feng Shui. Some books say 3000 years, while others 2500 and 2000 years. A website I visited recently even claims that Feng Shui originated in China 5000 years ago! 5000 years is an impressive and interesting claim considering people didn't even have proper houses to live in, let alone study or practice something as profound as Feng Shui. Which of these is correct?

The origins of this ancient science are quite murky. Some claim that Feng Shui has its origins in Chinese folklore, while some are of the idea that it is a numerical model from the sage Fu Xi. I have also read some books that say Feng Shui was formed by the combined knowledge of the Yi Jing, Chinese calendar and the Feng Shui Compass, which eventually developed into a science. Others say it is about symbols and decorations. Some people say it was the sage Fu Xi or King Wen, the founders of the Early Heaven and Later Heaven Ba Gua. Others say it came from the Lady of the Nine Heavens and the Yellow Emperor.

Which is it?!

It is not possible to exactly trace WHO developed Feng Shui in the first place – indeed, the term Feng Shui is in itself a relatively recent term, only coming into existence in the last 100 years or so.

It is clear from history that Feng Shui is not a 5000 year old science as some claim. Sophisticated Feng Shui methods were not used officially until the Tang Dynasty (618-907). Before that, it was only an art of selecting sites for capital cities, palaces or graves using very simple Yin and Yang methods. Even in the Tang Dynasty (around 1000 years ago), it wasn't really referred to as 'Feng Shui'. It was then known as the art of 'Kan Yu'.

FU XI

Next we come to the question of **WHERE**. Where did Feng Shui come from?

The simple answer is CHINA, of course. The real answer to the question is it depends on which system of Feng Shui we are discussing. Different systems of Feng Shui developed in different parts of China. Xuan Kong for example, was pioneered by Master Jiang Da Hong who came from the Zhe Jiang province of China. The Tan Yang Wu system of Xuan Kong has its roots in Shanghai.

From **WHEN** and **WHERE**, we move on to the question of **WHAT** is Feng Shui.

Kan

Now, often you hear people say that Feng Shui is about living in harmony with the environment. Feng Shui is NOT really an art of 'living in harmony' with the environment. I think this definition is too stereotypical. What do we exactly mean by 'living in harmony with' something anyway?

Yu

Feng Shui, at its core, is a study of Yin and Yang. I can just hear you say … WHAT? Just Yin and Yang? Yes, just Yin and Yang. Through the dynasties, the simple application of Yin and Yang evolved to incorporate many new findings. Patterns were compiled and later turned into formulas. This led to the rise of the many existing systems of Feng Shui.

It is more accurate and precise to say that Feng Shui is an art of assessing the qualities of Qi that converge at or affect a certain location in our environment and to ascertain its potential and shortcomings. As the influence of Qi in any given environment is governed by certain patterns calculable by formulae, we can assess the potential of Qi in reference to TIME and LOCATION.

This definition is supported by the ancient Chinese texts, where Feng Shui is classified under "Physiognomy of the Land" in the Chinese Five Arts. The Chinese Five Arts or Chinese Metaphysics are Mountain, Medical, Divination, Destiny and Physiognomy. The Art of Chinese Physiognomy includes areas like Face Reading, Palm Reading and of course, Feng Shui. The purpose of Feng Shui therefore is to foretell the fortune of the house (and its residents) through observations of the factors in our environment. Thus, it is not wrong to say that Feng Shui is 'House-Fortune Telling'.

Another misconception about WHAT Feng Shui is about is the idea that Feng Shui is all about promoting Health, Wealth and Prosperity or the very shallow definition of Feng Shui as being about the placement of objects or cures. If we must define Feng Shui as an art then Feng Shui is the art of harnessing the powers of the land, time and space, to benefit an individual's endeavours.

In recent time, there has been much confusion about Feng Shui that it has been reduced to this New Age concept of the art of placement. For practitioners and serious enthusiasts of Feng Shui, I believe it is important to provide a more dignified view of Feng Shui by ensuring that accurate information is available to unveil the What, Where, When, Why's of Feng Shui.

What is Feng Shui really about? Do you know?

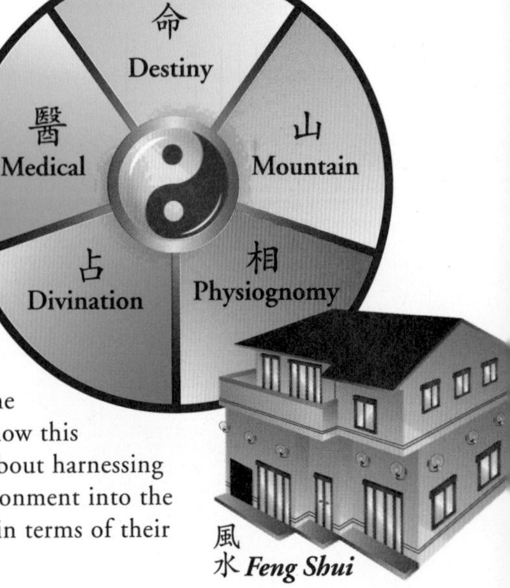

To the majority of people, if you ask them, they think that Feng Shui is nothing but the way they've designed their garden. Contrary to popular belief, Feng Shui is far from just decoration and interior design.

Feng Shui is about assessing the flow of Qi in a property and how this Qi affects the residents. It is about harnessing the Qi from the external environment into the home to benefit the residents in terms of their endeavors in life.

It is about how Yang Qi flows to and interacts with Yin Qi to give birth to new Qi – the interaction of Yin and Yang.

Yang Qi can be described as what is active and dynamic. The energy that helps us work and perform at peak. We can conceptualize this in general terms as 'wealth' or 'career' related energies. You have to work to get wealth and career success, right? Your Feng Shui assessment should include analyzing and enhancing the right kind of Qi that is needed to help achieve this end.

Yin Qi is passive, subtle and often inactive form of energy. Often people assume Yin is bad. This could not be further from the truth. Yin is only a 'form' of Qi, it is not to be judged as good or bad. Because Yin Qi is subtle, it plays a longer-term effect on people. Yin, passive Qi, often affects the areas of health, personality development and human relationships. Yin Qi affects how we feel and how we think and perceive things. That is why many Feng Shui practitioners term it as 'people luck'.

Yin Qi is the source of energies that protect and nurture you when you sleep and rest in a house. When you sleep, there is Yin Qi protecting you and if this is dispersed, you will lose your protection and will easily get sick. There are various forms of Yin Qi that will affect the character of a person. Some can make a person more caring and loving. While there are some that can make a person bitter and angry. Others make a person jealous and unkind. Thus, Feng Shui practitioners generalize Yin Qi also under love and marriage.

People are led to believe that it's the 'items' or the 'decor' they have around their house that create or manifest Qi.

Really, there is no magical trick. You cannot cultivate good Yin Qi (or Yang Qi) to bring love and romance by having a pair of mandarin ducks in the southwest part of your house. You also cannot harness 'wealth' Qi just by placing a dragon or a frog figurine in the corners of your house!

Knowing and understanding the characteristics of different types of Qi in a house (as presented by their immediate external environment in which their house is built) a Feng Shui practitioner can find a way to help people with Feng Shui techniques. This is in accordance with the concept of Yin and Yang balance.

Feng Shui has a bad reputation today because of the way people practice it. Commercialization of Feng Shui into a 12-step process, akin to roasting a turkey, has become the way to go these days. The practice of Feng Shui is not just about wealth, health and love. It is to help us achieve our endeavors, **whatever those might be.**

The Feng Shui Identity: What is Feng Shui?

When it comes to Feng Shui, I think there are generally three groups of people: the Believers, the Skeptics and the In-Betweens. The In-Betweens are those who are neither Believers nor absolute Skeptics.

As a consultant, naturally, I tend to meet people who believe in Feng Shui more. But I do not ignore the fact that amongst the general public, there are more Skeptics or In-betweens. Or, Believers who go to extremes.

The problem lies with the fact that there is so much hocus-pocus in this field, that one cannot help but feel a sense of misconception shrouding the practice. In fact, the art, science, study and practice of Feng Shui is a principled subject and no different from other traditional studies such as law, science, mathematics and accounting. Perhaps it simply has not had the benefit of practitioners who have sought to contextualize it as such. To put it in a better light so to speak.

Much of the confusion and skepticism stems from the absence of a definition for Feng Shui. Such a simple yet fundamental question "What is Feng Shui?" does not, it seems, have a firm answer.

Whenever I talk to members of the public or even my students, I get different answers. Here are some of the common ones:

1. Feng Shui is an Art of Placement
2. Feng Shui is Interior Design
3. Feng Shui is about decorating your house with good luck objects
4. Feng Shui is about living in harmony with nature
5. Feng Shui is about enhancing Wealth
6. Feng Shui is about enriching lives.

Which one of these is correct? Let's start with what Feng Shui is not. Feng Shui is definitely NOT the art of decorating your home with good luck objects NOR is it the so-called 'art of placement' of furniture and objects. Placement of objects and items is a new concept introduced in the 90s. It is what I call New Age Feng Shui.

Feng Shui is not about Interior Design. The furniture you buy, the color schemes and rich marble floors you choose are not part of Feng Shui theories or principles. Arranging furniture and choosing color schemes are best left to the expertise of an Interior Designer. You would never ask an architect or a land surveyor to advise you on interior design concepts. Then why ask a Feng Shui Master to undertake interior design work? Feng Shui and interior design are TWO different subjects altogether.

Many people today confuse 'Culture' with 'Feng Shui'. In the old days, Chinese good luck objects were used by wealthy individuals. But these objects were never used in the context of 'Feng Shui' but always as part of 'culture'.

Feng Shui is not about living in harmony with nature either. I find it odd when people say, "I want to live in harmony with nature, that's why I practice Feng Shui". If we were to really try and apply this principle in its literal sense, it would mean living in the forest, as close to harmony with nature as possible. While it is true that Feng Shui is about "harmonizing", the question is what is it we are trying to harmonize with?

So, having debunked what is NOT Feng Shui, I am sure you are curious to know – so what is it?

The Chinese have five categories of study in the world of Chinese Metaphysics (known as the Chinese Five Arts – Wu Shu), Feng Shui is classified under physiognomy of the living environment. The Five Arts are Mountain, Medical, Divination, Destiny and Physiognomy.

Physiognomy refers to observation of appearances through formulas and calculations in order to assess the potential and outcome of a person, or in this case, the outcome of a person living in a certain property.

Feng Shui is an art of "assessing" the quality of life through observations and analysis of the persons' living environment. Feng Shui in the old days was known as "Kan Yu" (the observation of the forces between Heaven and Earth). Only towards the end of the Qing Dynasty did the term "Feng Shui" come to be used unanimously to represent "Kan Yu".

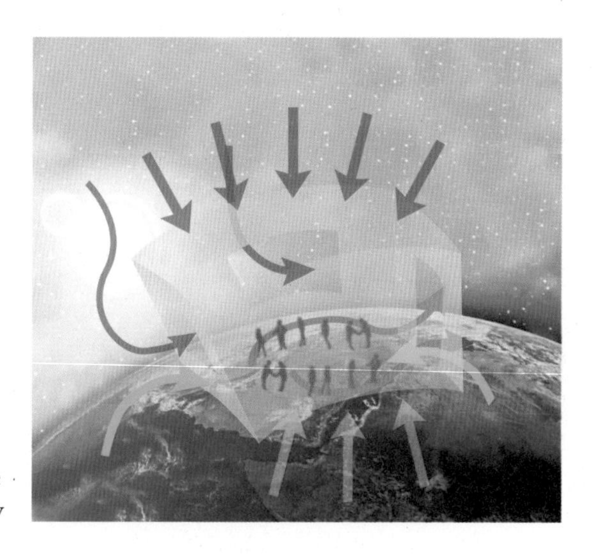

Feng Shui is a metaphysical science where one learns to recognize and tap into the Qi (cosmic energies) of the living environment to help endeavors in life. The study and presence of Qi is today recognized by Western medical doctors when it comes to acupuncture and acupressure. Not only do we want to harness the Qi, we also want to use it to help

specific goals in our everyday lives. Qi is a natural phenomenon of the living environment, it is rarely 'generated' by man- made objects like decorative items and designs.

Feng Shui is also a form of "forecasting" or divination. The nature of Qi is cyclical and as such, can be calculated. Practitioners of Feng Shui have learnt to assess outcomes based on the influence of Qi upon a particular living environment. If you know the types of Qi that will affect the environment in certain months of the year, you can prepare for the best or worst of the situation. Making informed decisions is in fact part of both Chinese Feng Shui AND Chinese Astrology. The "predictive" and forecasting part of Feng Shui is often neglected or unknown to many practitioners today.

Feng Shui is not just about being rich, finding the right husband or striking the lottery. It is not a miracle cure.

Now that you understand what Feng Shui truly is, try to approach it with a specific goal in mind because that is what it is best utilised for: to harness the Qi in your environment in order to achieve a certain goal.

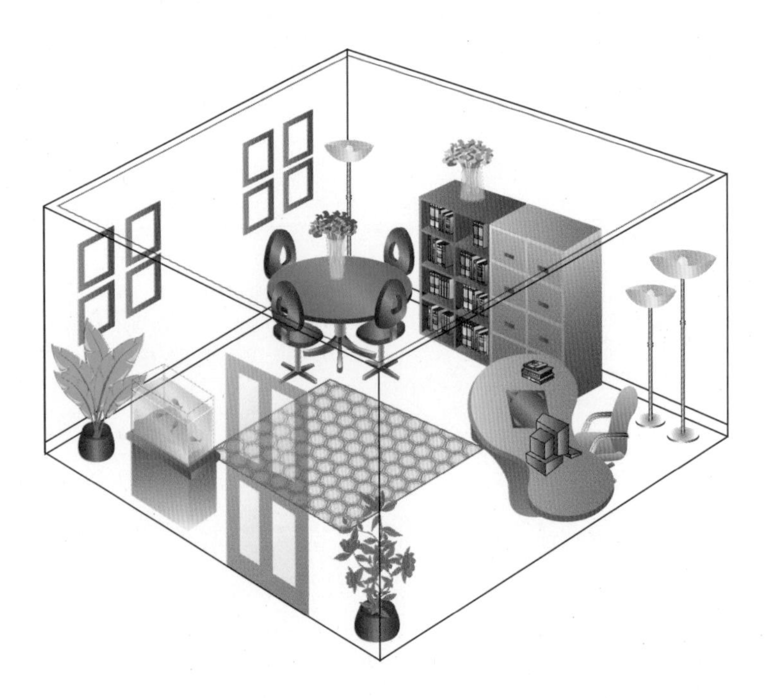

The Two Schools of Feng Shui

When Feng Shui was first used back in the ancient days, it was called the art of Kan Yu - the observation of forces between Heaven and Earth. Back then, the study of Feng Shui was not as developed and most of the information was still in its infancy. There was only one system and that system was based on the principles of Yin and Yang in conjunction with the 5 Elements.

Later on, through centuries of empirical research, statistical analysis and experiments, the Chinese sages and philosophers passed down their collective knowledge to disciples. Every generation, new findings were added and old theories redefined. The arrival of the Tang Dynasty was regarded as the prime era of Kan Yu. During those times, one particular ideology emerged as the most prominent. That was the San He system.

San He is regarded as the oldest form of Classical Feng Shui. This school places great emphasis on environmental features such as mountains, terrains and water. The direction, shape, flow and appearance of all these features in our environment become components for sophisticated formulae. Later on, a new ideology emerged – the San Yuan system, which is largely based on the mathematics and numerical logic of the Yi Jing.

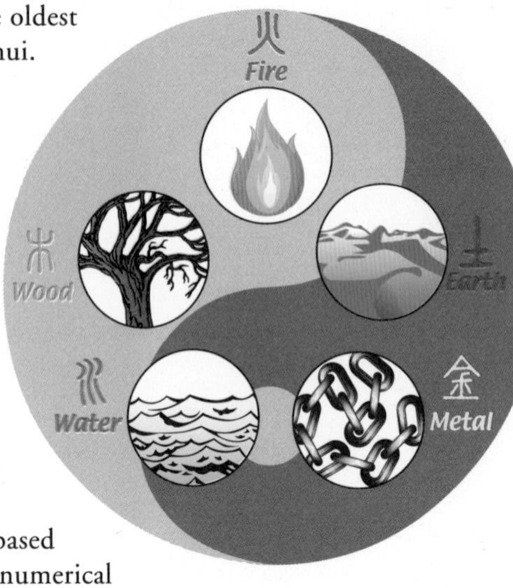

San Yuan was developed based on founding principles similar to San He. The main difference being that San Yuan placed more emphasis on the aspect of "Time" while San He focused more on the physiognomy, appearance, forms and flow of water in the environment.

Both these systems are authentic Classical Feng Shui systems, serving either corrective, constructive or predictive purposes. A practitioner uses Feng Shui to remedy existing problems (corrective), enhance wealth, health or relationships or to produce a particular outcome (constructive) or to predict future possibilities (predictive).

Although many of the schools or systems are rivals of one another, undoubtedly, there has always been mutual respect between them because they recognized that each had its own unique strengths and specialties.

When Feng Shui was first practised (presumably during Chou Dynasty 206BC – 219BC), there weren't any particular schools. There was only ONE type of Feng Shui and that used Forms and Yin and Yang of the Five Elements to determine the quality of the site. Later on, through their own study of the Yi Jing and practical experiences, practitioners began developing their own methodologies and discovered new theories. Due to the unique experiences of each practitioner, a number of different schools of thought sprang up. However, all of them based their theories on a sound understanding and the principles of Yi Jing.

It is important to note that Classical Feng Shui is not created based on psychology, superstition or positive thinking. Classical Feng Shui is a serious study of how the unseen energies in our living environment affect the people living or working in that particular area and in a certain period of time.

Perhaps you have heard of the Form School and Compass School. These two terms should not be used to describe the schools of Feng Shui as every classical or authentic school of Feng Shui uses Forms and Compass. If Feng Shui does not involve a FORMS and COMPASS reading, chances are it is not real Feng Shui!

From "San He" and "San Yuan", various sub-systems of Feng Shui are derived. Some of these divisions are:

- Xuan Kong 玄空 (aka Mysterious Subtleties, Time and Space School)
- Xuan Kong Fei Xing 玄空飛星 (popularly known as the Flying Stars School)
- Xuan Kong Da Gua 玄空大卦 (64 Hexagrams Method School)
- Xuan Kong Shui Fa 玄空水法 (Time and Space Water Method School)
- Zi Bai 紫白 (Purple White Flying Stars School)
- Major Wandering Stars School 大遊年
- Minor Wandering Stars School 小遊年
- San Yuan Dragon Gate Eight Formation School 三元龍門八局
- San He Luan Tou 三合巒頭 – (Environmental Appearance and Land Formations School)
- San He Shui Fa 三合水法 – (Water Methods School)
- Qi Men Dun Jia 奇門盾甲 – (Mystical Doorways and Magic Armour School)

Most Classical Feng Shui systems are derivatives of either the San He or San Yuan methodologies or of both. The Eight Life Aspirations (North = Career, South = Fame, SouthWest = Marriage) is NOT part of any Classical Schools of Feng Shui. Eight Life Aspirations has no foundation in either methodology, nor does it have any principles derived from the Yi Jing.

Undoubtedly, many enthusiasts of Feng Shui are confused by the conflicting theories of the different systems. The fact is, Classical Feng Shui schools do not always have 'conflicting' theories; they simply operate on different 'levels'.

Indeed, today, Classical Feng Shui is practised as "one" school. Masters and practitioners have learnt that by recognizing the strengths and uniqueness of each system, they can improve the quality of their work.

Easy Feng Shui for Sophisticated Living

How many people would like a simple solution that will bring about an immense change in the Feng Shui of their property? Probably everybody.

Me too. Honestly.

I would really love it if Feng Shui were a weekend do-it-yourself project that required nothing more than a couple of screws, a hammer and an electric drill. And possibly a simple diagram on what goes where.

However, the truth of the matter is that Feng Shui, like any science, requires a great deal of study and is not a weekend subject. The various systems of classical Feng Shui - San Yuan, San He, Xuan Kong, Ba Zhai are already an indication of how vast and rich the knowledge contained in Feng Shui is.

But people are always interested in something they can implement 'right NOW' and so, quick answers and quick fixes to problems that they are facing. It's sad that people are willing to trade quality for a quick fix that may not even work effectively.

Although there is no such thing as a quick fix, there are some simple methods in Feng Shui that you can implement, without requiring full scale renovations and an architect. The simplest method available to us is the 'Life Gua' method of Eight Mansions.

East Group 東命

Gua 卦	Sheng Qi 生氣	Tian Yi 天醫	Yan Nian 延年	Fu Wei 伏位	Huo Hai 禍害	Wu Gui 五鬼	Liu Sha 六煞	Jue Ming 絕命
Kan 坎 1 Water	South East	East	South	North	West	North East	North West	South West
Zhen 震 3 Wood	South	North	South East	East	South West	North West	North East	West
Xun 巽 4 Wood	North	South	East	South East	North West	South West	West	North East
Li 離 9 Fire	East	South East	North	South	North East	West	South West	North West

West Group 西命

Gua 卦	Sheng Qi 生氣	Tian Yi 天醫	Yan Nian 延年	Fu Wei 伏位	Huo Hai 禍害	Wu Gui 五鬼	Liu Sha 六煞	Jue Ming 絕命
Kun 坤 2 Earth	North East	West	North West	South West	East	South East	South	North
Qian 乾 6 Metal	West	North East	South West	North West	South East	East	North	South
Dui 兌 7 Metal	North West	South West	North East	West	North	South	South East	East
Gen 艮 8 Earth	South West	North West	West	North East	South	North	East	South East

First, you need to determine your Life Gua. Check the table included in the following pages to determine your Life Gua. The reference point is your Year of Birth.

Animal	Year of Birth	Gua Number for		Year of Birth	Gua Number for	
		Male	Female		Male	Female
Rat	1912 Water Rat 壬子 Ren Zi	7	8	1936 Fire Rat 丙子 Bing Zi	1	5
Ox	1913 Water Ox 癸丑 Gui Chou	6	9	1937 Fire Ox 丁丑 Ding Chou	9	6
Tiger	1914 Wood Tiger 甲寅 Jia Yin	5	1	1938 Earth Tiger 戊寅 Wu Yin	8	7
Rabbit	1915 Wood Rabbit 乙卯 Yi Mao	4	2	1939 Earth Rabbit 己卯 Ji Mao	7	8
Dragon	1916 Fire Dragon 丙辰 Bing Chen	3	3	1940 Metal Dragon 庚辰 Geng Chen	6	9
Snake	1917 Fire Snake 丁巳 Ding Si	2	4	1941 Metal Snake 辛巳 Xin Si	5	1
Horse	1918 Earth Horse 戊午 Wu Wu	1	5	1942 Water Horse 壬午 ren Wu	4	2
Sheep	1919 Earth Goat 己未 Ji Wei	9	6	1943 Water Goat 癸未 Gui Wei	3	3
Monkey	1920 Metal Monkey 庚申 Geng Shen	8	7	1944 Wood Monkey 甲申 Jia Shen	2	4
Rooster	1921 Metal Rooster 辛酉 Xin You	7	8	1945 Wood Rooster 乙酉 Yi You	1	5
Dog	1922 Water Dog 壬戌 Ren Xu	6	9	1946 Fire Dog 丙戌 Bing Xu	9	6
Pig	1923 Water Pig 癸亥 Gui Hai	5	1	1947 Fire Pig 丁亥 Ding Hai	8	7
Rat	1924 Wood Rat 甲子 Jia Zi	4	2	1948 Earth Rat 戊子 Wu Zi	7	8
Ox	1925 Wood Ox 乙丑 Yi Chou	3	3	1949 Earth Ox 己丑 Si Chou	6	9
Tiger	1926 Fire Tiger 丙寅 Bing Yin	2	4	1950 Metal Tiger 庚寅 Geng Yin	5	1
Rabbit	1927 Fire Rabbit 丁卯 Ding Mao	1	5	1951 Metal Rabbit 辛卯 Xin Mao	4	2
Dragon	1928 Earth Dragon 戊辰 Wu Chen	9	6	1952 Water Dragon 壬辰 Ren Chen	3	3
Snake	1929 Earth Snake 己巳 Ji Si	8	7	1953 Water Snake 癸巳 Gui Si	2	4
Horse	1930 Metal Horse 庚午 Geng Wu	7	8	1954 Wood Horse 甲午 Jia Wu	1	5
Sheep	1931 Metal Goat 辛未 Xin Wei	6	9	1955 Wood Goat 乙未 Yi Wei	9	6
Monkey	1932 Water Monkey 壬申 Ren Shen	5	1	1956 Fire Monkey 丙申 Bing Shen	8	7
Rooster	1933 Water Rooster 癸酉 Gui You	4	2	1957 Fire Rooster 丁酉 Ding You	7	8
Dog	1934 Wood Dog 甲戌 Jia Xu	3	3	1958 Earth Dog 戊戌 Wu Xu	6	9
Pig	1935 Wood Pig 乙亥 Yi Hai	2	4	1959 Earth Pig 己亥 Ji Hai	5	1

Animal	Year of Birth	Gua Number for		Year of Birth	Gua Number for	
		Male	Female		Male	Female
Rat	1960 庚子 Metal Rat Geng Zi	4	2	1984 甲子 Wood Rat Jia Zi	7	8
Ox	1961 辛丑 Metal Ox Xin Chou	3	3	1985 乙丑 Wood Ox Yi Chou	6	9
Tiger	1962 壬寅 Water Tiger Ren Yin	2	4	1986 丙寅 Fire Tiger Bing Yin	5	1
Rabbit	1963 癸卯 Water Rabbit Gui Mao	1	5	1987 丁卯 Fire Rabbit Ding Mao	4	2
Dragon	1964 甲辰 Wood Dragon Jia Chen	9	6	1988 戊辰 Earth Dragon Wu Chen	3	3
Snake	1965 乙巳 Wood Snake Yi Si	8	7	1989 己巳 Earth Snake Ji Si	2	4
Horse	1966 丙午 Fire Horse Bing Wu	7	8	1990 庚午 Metal Horse Geng Wu	1	5
Sheep	1967 丁未 Fire Goat Ding Wei	6	9	1991 辛未 Metal Goat Xin Wei	9	6
Monkey	1968 戊申 Earth Monkey Wu Shen	5	1	1992 壬申 Water Monkey Ren Shen	8	7
Rooster	1969 己酉 Earth Rooster Ji You	4	2	1993 癸酉 Water Rooster Gui You	7	8
Dog	1970 庚戌 Metal Dog Geng Xu	3	3	1994 甲戌 Wood Dog Jia Xu	6	9
Pig	1971 辛亥 Metal Pig Xin Hai	2	4	1995 乙亥 Wood Pig Yi Hai	5	1
Rat	1972 壬子 Water Rat Ren Zi	1	5	1996 丙子 Fire Rat Bing Zi	4	2
Ox	1973 癸丑 Water Ox Gui Chou	9	6	1997 丁丑 Fire Ox Ding Chou	3	3
Tiger	1974 甲寅 Wood Tiger Jia Yin	8	7	1998 戊寅 Earth Tiger Wu Yin	2	4
Rabbit	1975 乙卯 Wood Rabbit Yi Mao	7	8	1999 己卯 Earth Rabbit Ji Mao	1	5
Dragon	1976 丙辰 Fire Dragon Bing Chen	6	9	2000 庚辰 Metal Dragon Geng Chen	9	6
Snake	1977 丁巳 Fire Snake Ding Si	5	1	2001 辛巳 Metal Snake Xin Si	8	7
Horse	1978 戊午 Earth Horse Wu Wu	4	2	2002 壬午 Water Horse Ren Wu	7	8
Sheep	1979 己未 Earth Goat Ji Wei	3	3	2003 癸未 Water Goat Gui Wei	6	9
Monkey	1980 庚申 Metal Monkey Geng Shen	2	4	2004 甲申 Wood Monkey Jia Shen	5	1
Rooster	1981 辛酉 Metal Rooster Xin You	1	5	2005 乙酉 Wood Rooster Yi You	4	2
Dog	1982 壬戌 Water Dog Ren Xu	9	6	2006 丙戌 Fire Dog Bing Xu	3	3
Pig	1983 癸亥 Water Pig Gui Hai	8	7	2007 丁亥 Fire Pig Ding Hai	2	4

- Please note that the date for the Chinese Solar Year is Feb 4.
  This means that if you were born in Feb 2 of 2002, you belong to the previous year 2001.
- Male Gua 5 assume Gua 2. Female Gua 5 assume Gua 8.

Now, you will notice that from your Life Gua, you are either a East group or West group person. Some clients have asked me, why are there no 'North and South' Groups. You see these are just names to demarcate the Greater and Lesser Yin transformation of the Tai Ji. They do not literally represent directions. East Group is the Yang group while the West Group is Yin.

East Group Guas include 1, 3, 4 and 9. Those who are Guas 2, 6, 7 and 8 are in the West Group.

Now, refer to the following diagrams for a quick reference of the Auspicious and Inauspicious compass directions of the East and West Group.

West Group

Inauspicious 凶

Auspicious 吉

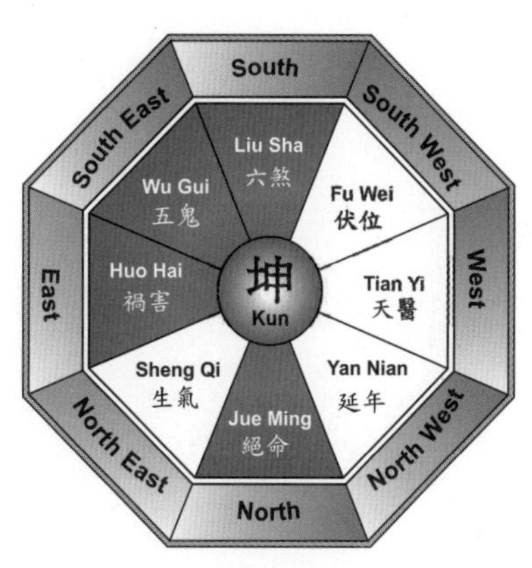

Kun Gua #2 (earth)

Qian Gua #6 (metal)

Dui Gua #7 (metal)

Gen Gua #8 (earth)

East Group

Kan Gua #1 (water)

Zhen Gua #3 (wood)

Xun Gua #4 (wood)

Li Gua #9 (fire)

Each direction is governed by a Star. In the Chinese texts, these are called the "Wandering Sars".

Sheng Qi 生氣 (Life Generating), Tian Yi 天醫 (Heavenly Doctor), Yan Nian 延年 (Longevity) and Fu Wei 伏位 (Stability) are Auspicious Stars. The Inauspicious Stars are Huo Hai 禍害 (Mishaps), Wu Gui 五鬼 (Five Ghost), Liu Sha 六煞 (Six Killings) and Jue Ming 絕命 (Life Diminishing).

Here is your quick fix: Avoid the Huo Hai, Wu Gui, Liu Sha and Jue Ming sectors for important areas like the bedroom, kitchen, study and Main Door. Try to have your bedroom or study in the auspicious direction!

See, didn't need a drill for that now did you?

Qi Tapping

There are three crucial factors to look at when assessing Feng Shui. Whatever else you may consider, make sure these three items are at the top of your 'To Be Checked' list.

The first is the Main Door. It would be ideal to have your main door facing one of your favorable directions - this is measured by standing inside your home, facing out.

Inside looking out

Now, you need to figure out what it is that you feel you need to improve or enhance. No point looking to tap Qi if you don't know what Qi it is you want to tap in the first place right? Do bald people perm their hair? No, because they don't have any hair to begin with. So don't just tap Qi without knowing why you're tapping it for.

If your focus in life at this point is more towards wealth creation or in line with improving your career, use the Sheng Qi direction. If you are buying or renting a house, then look for one that has the main door facing this direction.

Now, where you sleep is the next most important thing: so put the bedroom second on your checklist. If you want to improve your health, get in shape quickly or receive help from your colleagues at work, I recommend sleeping in the Tian Yi or Heavenly Doctor direction.

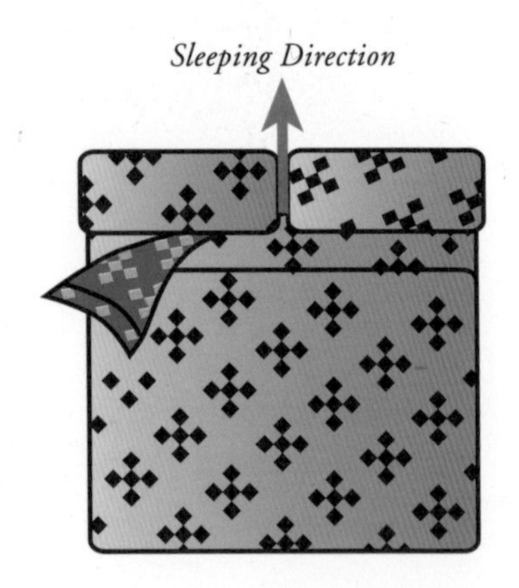

A common misconception beginners make is to measure the facing of the feet as the sleeping direction. It is actually measured from the headboard; the direction your head points to when you are sleeping.

Position your bed in such a way that it taps INTO your good directions. Of course when you are repositioning your bed, do take note of the basic principles of room arrangement. For example, even though you may be sleeping in your favorable direction, you should still avoid sleeping under an overhead beam or positioning your bed in such a manner that the room door opens up directly onto your bed.

Now, what about the work desk in the study or office? Make sure your work desk allows you to FACE the direction that benefits your position or goals. For example, if your work involves dealing with people - sales, marketing or public relations activity, use the Yan Nian (Longevity) direction. This direction helps promote relationships and foster good understanding and communication. Tapping into this direction helps you achieve these goals and will inadvertently support you in your career.

Should your love life and relationships require some improvements, then the Yan Nian direction is your best bet Qi.

Finally, choose your stars (or directions), wisely. Even though the Sheng Qi direction may be 'good' or the best, it may not necessarily be what you need. You will need to exercise some discretion in deciding what is best suited to your situation in life and tailor this to your goals.

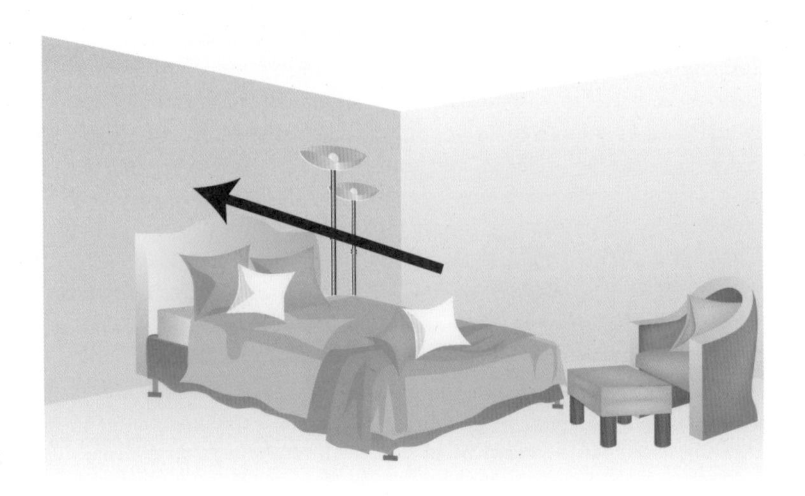

And please do not be too paranoid when applying this Life Gua methodology. I have had people going so far as to tailor their toilets to cater for a good direction when they are using the WC. A good acid test when assessing whether a living environment is required to face a good direction is to see how much time you will be spending there - a good rule of thumb is 30 minutes everyday. If it is less than 30 minutes, don't spend needless time worrying about it!

It's a Bird, It's a Plane – It's a House For Sale

A few days ago, I was driving to a friend's birthday party with my school friend Alex. On the way there, we were discussing a house that he had put up for sale for some time now. He was dismayed. It just didn't seem to sell even though there were many inquiries. He told me, as a last resort, he had decided to paste a picture of a 'bird' on the house's address plate as a means to sell it faster. I had to slam on the brakes to avoid hitting the car in front of me.

'A bird!' I exclaimed. 'A bird?'

'It's a Feng Shui technique to sell houses,' he proudly proclaimed.

'Which direction does this special bird fly?' I asked, unable to contain my curiosity.

'Err·.hee hee..well, no special direction. I think THAT could be the problem. The bird might have been placed in the wrong direction.'

Yes, THAT was the problem I thought to myself.

Not the overgrown weeds in the yard or the peeling paint of the house. Or the leaking roof. Or the fact that the house was a wreck and it had been left unattended for almost a year and in a less than upmarket neighbourhood.

But my friend Alex was adamant that it was the direction of the 'Feng Shui' bird he painted that is causing a hiccup to his intended sale.

'So, no takers for the house yet?' I asked him. 'No lah, all of them came, saw and left, saying that they would get back to me. But no news so far.'

'What do you think, Joey? Do you think you can help me with some adjustment to the 'bird' direction?' he finally asked me.

I decided to share with him my all-time killer secret technique for selling houses. This is where my expertise in real estate sales kicked in – no I haven't changed my vocation but read on. You will soon see why my mastery of the real estate game leaves many bird-painting friends awe struck.

The real secret Feng Shui technique of selling houses is to put up a FOR SALE sign to begin with. And here is the real magic, to sell it faster - put another sign below that says - 20% BELOW market price!'

Change that percentage as you see fit until the house is sold. And if that sign is HUGE, the better the 'Feng Shui' of your house as prospective buyers will line up to offer you money for this house with good 'Feng Shui'.

If only I could charge for common sense advice, I would have retired by now!

There is no magic Feng Shui formula by which pasting a painting of a bird on the house address will sell your land or house faster. If your house has 'real' good Feng Shui, buyers will find it more appealing; but good Feng Shui has nothing to do with a picture of a bird.

When a house has good Feng Shui, the Qi in the property is pleasant - visitors immediately find themselves attracted to the house and in certain cases, may even feel very comfortable in the house as soon as they enter.

I cannot say for certain where this 'bird picture' idea originated from as there is no reference to this in even Chinese culture. It may very well have started off as something valid before morphing into its present curious form. Maybe there was an old saying that if a property has birds and other forms of life, it has good Qi - perhaps this is where the idea was derived from.

There are of course, houses that can be particularly difficult to sell. Those with a Main Door directly facing a T- junction or a lamp post, where the Qi is fierce or not conducive. Most house buyers these days are somewhat Feng Shui savvy - they are going to know that such a structure is not good. Even without any knowledge about Feng Shui, common sense will tell you that having cars rushing towards your door day and night is hardly a good way to live.

And if you walk into a house that looks dark, dingy and overly 'Yin', you're obviously not going to find yourself too attracted to it. This goes for all those houses where the trees are so thick as to almost block out the sunlight.

If you encounter such a situation, keep in mind that if the particular area is also within a palace that has the 2, 4, 7, 9 stars - this could lead to a Yin Formation in Flying Star Feng Shui. The effects can include hallucinations or apparitions; traditionally also known as the neighbourhood's fabled haunted houses.

Also, watch out for houses with an imbalanced land shape, triangular or skewed at an odd angle. They face trouble in retaining Qi.

If you are selling your house, try these techniques: Cut the grass, pull out the weeds, give it a new coat of paint and do up the cracks and leaks. No one is going to buy a house that you yourself would not think of living in.

Location, Location, Location.

Master Lee, a famous master in Hong Kong, once made an interesting comment that has proven to be a golden nugget to me over the years. 'Never underestimate the power of location', he told me.

Facing a good direction may be helpful but being IN the right location AND facing a good direction spurs on the positive effects. Of course, this works just as negatively in the other direction - being in a disadvantaged location in the house may very well negate the good effects of facing your good direction.

This is why I constantly stress the importance of positioning your Main Door - the Qi mouth - in the right location in addition to it facing the correct direction. You want it to receive the best possible quality of Qi in your home and facing a favorable direction further amplifies this effect.

You may often hear that decor or colour is THE thing to look out for if you want to enhance your Feng Shui. Not true. Keep in mind the most crucial factors will always be direction and locations; the colour of your walls and curtains will not be influencing the Qi within your home.

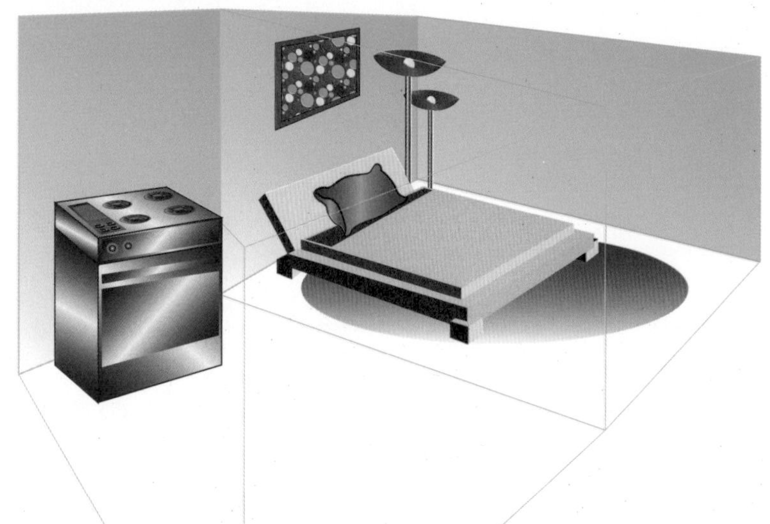

Often, many enthusiasts of Feng Shui imagine that changing the internal Feng Shui of their homes will change their fortunes overnight. Thus, the way they sit, the direction of their bed and the décor of the house in general, are all scrutinized from top to bottom to ensure 'perfection'.

The Big Picture is overlooked invariably.

If you take a closer look at the events that have come to pass in your life, the events you have undergone and the opportunities life has presented you, these next few items will definitely have played a crucial role in all of them:

- The water and mountain positions you have in the vicinity of your home.
- The location and direction of your main door.
- The location of your bedroom and
- The location of your kitchen.

Indeed, the influence of 'location', be it in a city, a suburb, a township, within your house, the rooms and the location of our desks is a powerful factor that shapes our lives. At times, we may not even realize just how powerful this effect can be as it influences us over an extended period of time.

Before even checking anything internally, we need to first check and fix the main flaws in the external picture. Where is our building located (within the suburb or housing estate)? What are the nearby mountain ranges and main roads that govern the main Qi of the area?

If you have studied Feng Shui, you may have heard the term Luan Tou which is also known as Forms. Forms refer to the mountain ranges and rivers in our environment. Environmental factors are powerful. They can often nudge us just a little bit and then a little bit more until we take a good look around and behind us and realize that we have gone completely off course! And often, this can be detrimental to the Feng Shui goals that we have set out for ourselves.

A property should be ideally tapping into the beneficial resources of the surrounding land and then, at the same time, we tailor the internal Qi to fit our own lives.

Some of you may feel a bit skeptical, especially if you have lived all your life in the same place. But environmental features do matter and they do have a pronounced effect on your life. Ignorance in this case may become a setback in your endeavours to seek the beneficial effects of good Feng Shui. Assess the environment and see if the scales may be tipped towards the positive or negative and then manage it from there.

As a quick guide, here are the questions you want to ask yourself to assess your current Feng Shui conditions:

1. Where is my house located? Within my housing estate or suburb, am I in the Northern sector or Eastern sector? What are the various mountain and water locations within my vicinity that I most often see?

2. Are these environmental features good or are they having a negative impact on my home?

3. What are their influences? Is the mountain in the right location in relation to my property? Is the water position correct? Is the road in and out of my property area correct?

Maybe you've been fortunate and the area in which you live in has been a positive, energizing influence. Then again, maybe there are some negative features in the environment that you haven't taken into account till now. Take a close and objective look.Check for incoming roads, incoming mountains, mountain ranges, taller buildings, negative and environmental features. These lay the foundation for good or bad Feng Shui in your property.

It may often be natural and easier to get carried away with interior Feng Shui. But if you just stopped and looked around, the problem may not be the colour of your door or where your door is, but what is OUTSIDE your door.

But My Teacher Says ...

Throughout my experience as a master trainer of Feng Shui, I have found that there is this penchant for students to blindly follow something they have learnt or read or heard without really questioning the theory or the 'why's' behind it.

Confusion amongst students is often caused by the 'you say this but my teacher says or this book I read says that' line of questioning. Often I find students expect me to confirm that their original understanding of the application (no matter how wrong it may have been) was correct or they want me to prove that their author/teacher was wrong.

Many students today seem to be easily awed by a teacher or an author's fame and celebrity status. They overlook the information presented and forget that any Feng Shui knowledge needs to still be verified and supported by the fundamentals of Feng Shui. An unhealthy habit and practice is formed when such information becomes the gospel truth – something that is not to be questioned.

Students are, of course, in a difficult predicament when teachers brush them aside claiming 'they have eaten more salt than you have eaten rice', a Chinese saying meant to indicate that one has more experience and so therefore, should be kow-towed to. But remember, what we learn from a teacher may be one view of the principle or theory but to truly excel, a student needs to look beyond blindly taking what a teacher says is the gospel truth. One should not be afraid to question and ask why. It is not enough that you take 'that's just the way it is, take my word for it' answers as satisfactory.

Although experience is an important factor, it can never fully replace a sound understanding behind the theory. It is crucial that any teacher is able to reason out and explain his formula to verify his experience. In the same vein, an academic ivory tower approach alone will not fill in the gaps left by inexperience in practice.

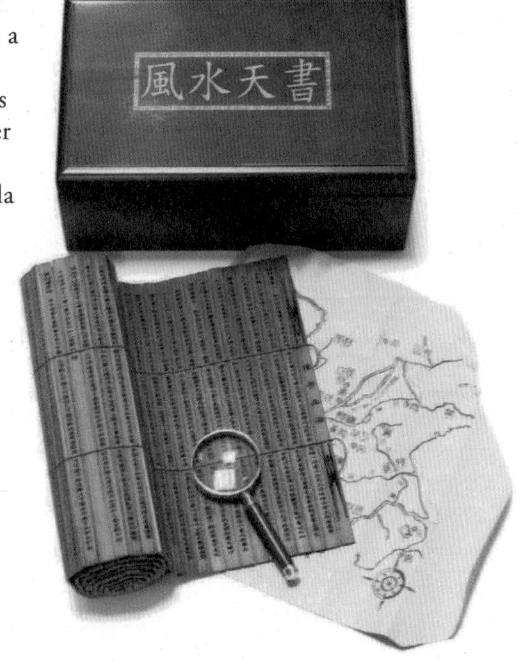

I call this the Yin and Yang of Feng Shui; one will not do without the other.

When studying any subject, including Classical Feng Shui, we need to learn to assess the information presented, research the theory and think independently before formulating a conclusion. Each application must be backed by sound theory and understanding. Simply learning the technique and not grasping the theories that go into making it up is not learning Feng Shui the smart way. It's not even learning Feng Shui.

The most important two questions that any student of Feng Shui should always ask themselves are: Do you know the WHY's behind the theories that are taught to you? If you know why, do you know HOW to use them?

Always, and I mean always, ask your teacher to explain the why's behind the theory or look at the explanation provided by an author for a certain theory or principle.

Check that a teacher has a clear understanding of the theory and application and that his explanation is both logical and supported by classical text. Also, ask about his experience in the application of this formula in his practice and whether it achieved the desired results. If your teacher cannot clearly offer you an explanation or answer, you may very well be up the wrong creek without a paddle on a boat heading to nowhere.

If the answer revolves around a reference to classical texts without any references to clear Feng Shui principles or fundamentals, you also need to be careful.

Wait a minute you're thinking - how can even classical texts be wrong? Aren't these the origins of Feng Shui principles?

The history of most classical texts and their very age alone can lead to inconsistencies. Although many parts within these classical texts are usable, other sections are unusable and only an experienced teacher who has researched the fundamentals behind these theories will know if they are accurate or otherwise.

Water formulas are a good example of this. I have had desperate phone calls from people on the verge of bankruptcy, tycoons who have been reduced to selling their houses and practitioners who have blindly applied the formulas without looking into the theory behind them and caused their clients to run into serious problems. Water formulas from the ancient texts may be powerful, but many people are easily taken in by the supposed potential they hold.

Chinese texts write in length about how effective water formulas can be but it remains that until today, there is no concrete empirical evidence that they are 100 percent as powerful or do what they claim to do. To add spice to the confusing soup, the application is also extremely complex.

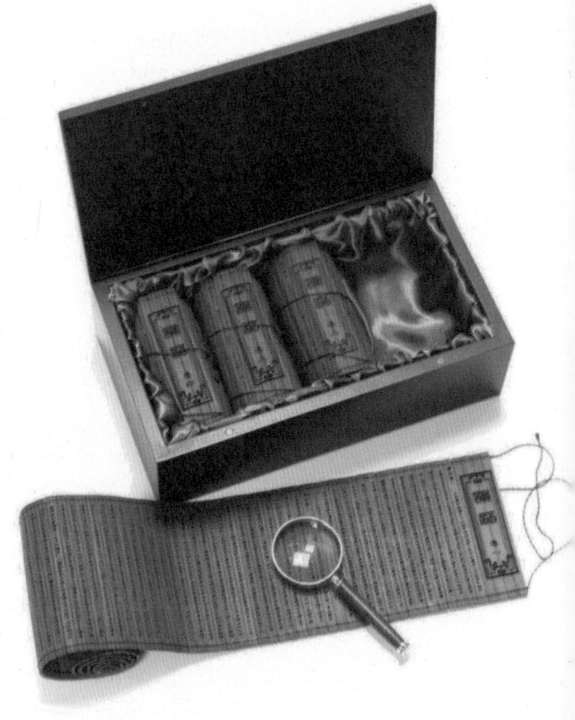

Think about it - If it really were so easy, why isn't every Feng Shui Master a billionaire? Wouldn't their children and family members be the first to benefit from their knowledge?

So, the next time you practice something as simple as the Eight Mansions (Ba Zhai), ask yourself: WHY is the formula as such? For example, if you are a Gua #2 person, why is your Sheng Qi North East? Do you know what the element of Sheng Qi is? What really is Sheng Qi? Is it a star? Or a body of Qi? What's the difference between two people who are Gua #2, both using the same North East Sheng Qi direction? Will they now enjoy the same level of success? If not, why not? How do we activate Sheng Qi or Tian Yi other than 'facing' that direction? Which classical text is it from? Why is the Gua of the house not used?

The best way to learn is by asking yourself the difficult questions. You are your best teacher. It is the fastest way to study and de-mystify Feng Shui. Asking leads you to the right answer with a purpose. When I teach Feng Shui, I encourage my students to think on their own. The ultimate conclusion has to be reached by the student after looking at the available information and questioning the theories – I am merely a guide in their search for the answers.

I do acknowledge and understand that old school teachers normally are not in the habit of explaining too much. This was evident when I was studying in Hong Kong. But sometimes, this is because the old school teachers are experience-based, and have studied for 20 years through a Master-Disciple relationship before graduating. Equally, it is because they expect their students to 'see' the answers by thinking and doing their own research.

In today's world, nobody has the luxury of time. That is why I encourage students to learn and study, research theories on their own. Teachers should help by explaining the why's and not just the how's. The Western education system is good in this aspect – a point sorely lacking in traditional Chinese learning methodologies. After all what is the use of teaching your students if they then become 'dependant' on you for knowledge and cannot think on their own?

Do not be misled by the phrase 'my teacher says this and my teacher says that'. It does not matter what your teacher says, what does matter is if you understand what they are saying and if the principles are correct upon further investigation. Seek out the reasoning behind the theory and do not be blinded simply because of your faith in any school, teacher or system. You owe it to yourself.

Date Selection Frenzy

A friend complained to me recently about the headache he was facing with his new office. His contractor it seemed had failed to finish the renovation works in time, resulting in his official opening not being timely and missing the 'auspicious hour'(吉時).

Many people assume that Date Selection is merely selecting an auspicious date and time for ground breaking or renovating a house. Others believe it's just a formality to ensure 'auspicious' good tidings for events to proceed smoothly. There are also extreme instances of what I call 'Date Selection Frenzy' where a good date is sought for just about everything and anything under the sun.

To the layperson, date selection appears not only complex but tedious as well. Every month, there are good and bad days – but then again, good days and bad days for WHAT exactly?

There are two categories of Date Selection:

- For Yin House – specific dates are selected for Ground Breaking, Burial, Opening the Mountain and Establishing the Facing (Kai Shan Li Xiang 開山立向)

- For Yang House – specific dates for ground breaking, renovations, move in dates, installing a cure.

In addition to these, Date Selection can also be used for performing certain activities such as signing a contract, opening a business, moving the bed or traveling. This is what is commonly known as activity or action-based Date Selection.

There are many methods of Date Selection – it is almost a school of study in itself. They include:

- Dong Gong (Grand Master Dong Method) 董公
- Qi Men Dun Jia (Mystical Doorways and Magic Armour) 奇門遁甲
- Tian Xing (Heavenly Stars) 天星
- San He (Three Combinations) 三合
- Dou Sou (28 Constellations) 斗首
- Ba Zi (Eight Characters, Four Pillars) 八字
- Zi Bai Jiu Xing (Purple White Nine Stars) 紫白九星
- Xuan Kong Da Gua (Xuan Kong 64 Hexagrams Method) 玄空大卦
- Wu Tu (Black Rabbit) 烏兔
- Shen Sha (Gods and Killings method) 神煞

Each school or system has its own strengths and weaknesses that also serve to highlight how complex or simple each system may be. Some are exclusively used for Yin House Feng Shui, while others for Yang House and still others for certain specific activities.

The trick here lies in using the right method for the given situation and this in itself has been the cause for much debate over the centuries within the numerous schools of thought on Date Selection.

Personally, I base most of my work on a 'main system' with a sub-system to back up the reading as and where necessary. However, where activity-based selection is concerned, my personal favorite has to be Xuan Kong's Zi Bai Jiu Xing – the Purple White Nine Stars method.

All good practitioners always have a pet system, so to speak and mine is Xuan Kong. The Xuan Kong Zi Bai system offers a unique complementary system to the usual Xuan Kong Feng Shui that I do. But for non-activity based Date Selection, I still use BaZi, Dong Gong and Dou Sou as the main system.

DATE SELECTION is a study by itself.

Date Selection is a study by itself. When a Feng Shui practitioner undertakes Date Selection, its purpose is crucial to the whole process. What activity are we selecting this date for? Remember, every day has a set of Qi and it can be used to help activate or adversely, destroy an endeavour at that point.

A Hoo Hah Over Period 8

Come February 4th 2004, the Feng Shui 'calendar' enters what is known as Period 8. February 3rd 2004 will mark the end of what is known as Period 7.

Now, watching the TV or reading books on Feng Shui these days gives people the impression that come February 4th 2004, at precisely 7:58pm, the sky will fall in, the world as we know it, will come to an end, rich tycoons will suddenly become poor paupers as their good luck 'expires' and the Qi drains from their homes. At the stroke of 7:59 pm on February 4th 2004, anyone who has enjoyed good luck in the past few years will suddenly 'lose' all that good luck in the space of one minute.

Now, Period 8 is an important transition where Feng Shui is concerned, but it has been exploited and used to scare people into buying items for 'renewing the luck' of their home or forcing them to undertake huge and massive renovations to renew the expired Qi.

Let's get a little background on Period 8.

In Feng Shui, the element of TIME is crucial. No home or office enjoys good luck or bad luck forever. The factor of Time is an important element that must be taken into consideration when performing a Feng Shui analysis.

All Classical schools of Feng Shui (San Yuan, San He, Xuan Kong and even Ba Zhai) refer to the Time factor in their classical texts. No Feng Shui assessment can be considered comprehensive unless the concept of Time is considered. The Time factor of course receives a different emphasis, depending on the system of Feng Shui. Different systems of Feng Shui use different methods of analyzing Time.

CYCLE 元	PERIOD 運	YEAR 年	GUA 卦
上 UPPER	1	1864 - 1883	Kan 坎
	2	1884 - 1903	Kun 坤
	3	1904 - 1923	Zhen 震
中 MIDDLE	4	1924 - 1943	Xun 巽
	5	1944 - 1963	-
	6	1964 - 1983	Qian 乾
下 LOWER	7	1984 - 2003	Dui 兑
	8	2004 - 2023	Gen 艮
	9	2024 - 2043	Li 離

The concept of the changeover in periods, say from Period 7 to Period 8, originates from Flying Star Feng Shui or Xuan Kong Fei Xing, an extremely popular and potent system of Time Dimension Feng Shui practiced in Hong Kong, Taiwan, Singapore and Malaysia.

In Flying Star Feng Shui, TIME is divided into 20-Year cycles. Each cycle of 20 years is known as a 'Period'. There are 9 Periods in total which cover a span of 180 years, known as a Grand Cycle.

The Periods describe the cyclical pattern of Qi. Different types of Qi have different strengths and weaknesses depending on the Period in reference. It is utilizing these cyclical patterns that Feng Shui practitioners can assess the 'timeliness' of certain types of Qi and determine how the Qi present in the property will affect the residents in a certain Period or over time.

Period 7 was governed by the Dui Gua Trigram (#7). Dui represents the West, young women, technology, communication and metaphysics. In Period 7, all these aspects saw a heightened focus and advancement.

On February 4 2004, we entered Period 8. There will be a shift in energies and the Gen Trigram (#8) will take over. The energies of Gen will shift the focus to young men, mountains and overall stability. These are basic attributes of the Gen trigram.

From the countless emails I received in the run up to February 4th 2004 and the numerous questions during seminars and public talks, it's clear that many people have an UNFOUNDED FEAR about this change.

I have been asked many times by house owners if their houses will 'instantly lose Qi' with the transition. Or they fear that the #7 Star, the Wealth Star in Period 7, and which brought about good fortune will revert back to its original negative self and bring about its destructive effects - injuries, blood related accidents, robberies and violence. Many of these house owners were also considering 'changing the Period' of their house or office.

My advice to these house owners and to you would be to...relax! This is a simple case of people being afraid of what they do not understand. A little information can be a dangerous thing.

For starters, the 'instant bad luck' concept is a case of things being blown out of proportion. There is definitely a shift in the Qi pattern but bear in mind that Qi moves in a CYCLICAL fashion. Shifts in this case are gradual and not immediate. There is no such thing as an instant change in vitality and Qi strength when a Period transition occurs. We're not talking about instant noodles here.

Experienced Feng Shui practitioners will have already seen that the #7 Star began to lose its vitality even as far back as year 2000. A skilled Feng Shui practitioner would have already begun advising his clients to tap into the Period 8 stars before February 4th 2004.

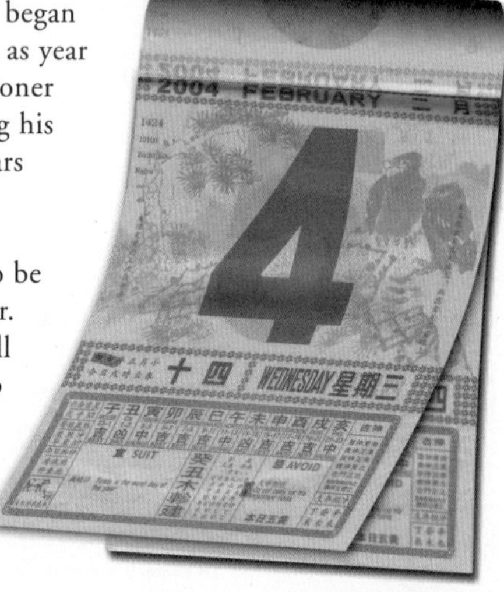

Not all houses in Period 7 need to be changed to a Period 8 house either. Even some Period 6 charts can still be beneficial in Period 8. Do keep in mind that a change of period requires extensive work and involves serious renovations, which include the changing the roof and new main doors.

By the same token, some Period 8 houses present many disappointingly unusable areas. Remember also that even if a house has a good chart, it still has to be supported by suitable forms in the environment.

Keep in mind it is not the Period of the house that matters; it is how the stars in the house are managed and deployed to the benefit of the residents. Every chart in every Period has an equal number of stars in the 9 Palaces. It is up to the skill of a Feng Shui practitioner to activate or deactivate certain areas and to make the house beneficial to the residents. Like all things in Feng Shui, I like to tell my clients and students: make the best of what you have and don't let what you can't do stop you from improving things with what you CAN do.

It's Period 8 – What Now?

Now that you know there's no Hoo-Hah or fear of the sky falling in with the arrival of Period 8, the question is how do you make the best of this change?

Now, in the early stages of Period 8, we will see the #7 Star entering the 'Retreating Qi' stage. At this point it slowly (not instantly) reverts back to its original evil nature. However, unless you have negative environmental features that activate or quicken the negative aspects of the #7 star, things would be just fine. There is still some time left to make any changes you're planning to undertake.

First, obtain the Flying Star Chart for your home. You need to know the exact Facing direction of your home, which you can obtain by using a compass or with a Luo Pan if you want a more accurate reading, then plot the Flying Star Chart. Whereas in Period 7, we tapped into the #7 Star as the Wealth star, we similarly need to find the location of the #8 Star in the house's Flying Star chart and tap into it for Period 8. If the house's internal and external factors are conducive, you will enjoy the same (if not better) fortunes in the coming Period.

Take a look at the location of your main door and the stars in that sector. If the Facing Star is a #7 or #6, then you need to make some changes. However, if your door has the good fortune of being located where there's a facing #8 or #9 Stars, then there is no need to do anything. You will have good fortune in Period 8.

A CHANGE can often do more DAMAGE than GOOD

Ideally, you should locate your Main Door and any other doors where the prosperous #8 and #9 Facing Stars are located. Important bedrooms should be placed where the #8, #9 or #1 Sitting Stars are found.

If your home does not have doors opening in the #8 or #9 Facing Stars, then consider activating it by placing a Water feature such as an aquarium in the area. Finally, keep in mind the Environment. The good Facing Stars (#8 and #9) need the right forms as well to be activated. Use External and Internal water and mountains to activate the stars accordingly. See, no problem to it really.

Now, I want to correct a very important 'idea' that a lot of people have about what they should do in Period 8. It is an incorrect assumption that many people make when they jump to the conclusion that they need to change their house to Period 8 to enjoy good Feng Shui. Be very careful when you do decide to switch over to a Period 8 house. A change can often do more damage than good; especially in cases where the environment is not supportive of your home.

An example of this would be a North 1 house in Period 7. When it enters Period 8, the #8 Facing Star in the front of the property now benefits the occupants of the residence. If you were to simply renovate this house, you may lose out on this benefit.

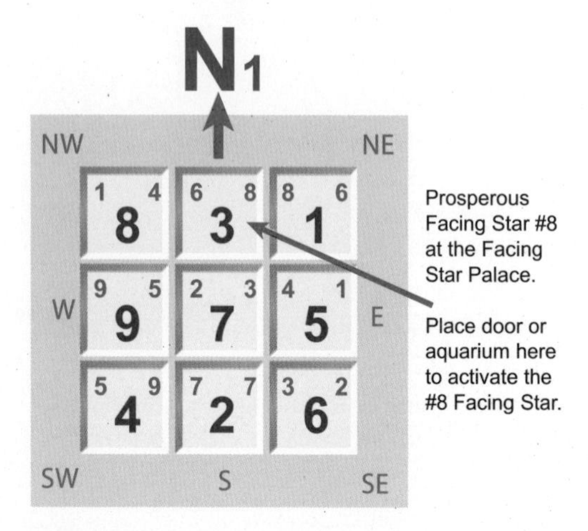

A North 1 Period 7 house chart.

The properous #8 Facing Star is already at the Facing Palace.

This house will automatically do better in period 8. (No Period change needed)

Doing it yourself is an option if you don't mind a certain amount of experimentation. But I recommend having your house plans audited by a Professional Feng Shui Consultant if you do plan to make any major changes or renovations to your home. You may not even need a full consultation if all you are looking to do is address the change of period issue.

For more information or to learn what to do with Period 8, you may wish to purchase a copy of my DVD presentation: Feng Shui for Period 8. *http://masteryacademy.com/education/period8/index.asp*

The Under Water Taboo

Feng Shui is neither magical nor mysterious. It is a science. It works as a natural consequence of consistently applying basic ‘fundamentals of the I-Ching (Yi Jing)’: the principles of balance, equilibrium (Yin/Yang), Qi, Trigrams and the Five Elements.

Feng Shui is about the application of a few simple fundamental principles. When practiced correctly and applied in your home, it can often lead to success. Failure in Feng Shui is often attributable to a certain judgmental errors, caused by misguidance or commonly, the wrong interpretation of the fundamentals.

Now, fundamentals are just that – fundamentals. There are no NEW fundamentals. I often get a little suspicious of students who say, "I've found a new fundamental." It’s like someone proclaiming they have found a new way to manufacture real historical artifacts.

This was exactly what one of my readers proclaimed when he wrote to me and asked me whether he should get rid of his aquarium. His house was rather unique in that it had the living room above the dining room and he had his aquarium in the living room. He had heard that it was a Feng Shui no-no to have water situated above you. Apparently, this denoted a dangerous situation.

Aquarium in the second floor. Bad Feng Shui?

He proceeded into a long explanation of how he had heard that having water above you is unfavourable or negative since in the I-Ching (or Yi Jing, Book of Changes), having water on top is a sign of suffocation and danger. He was convinced that all fundamental Feng Shui stemmed from the theories of the I-Ching, so this must be an evident taboo in Feng Shui.

He couldn't reason out why this was so. But he was obviously worried since this 'advice' seemed to specify 'danger' if one has water located above.

I reassured him and let him know that it was perfectly fine to have water in the living room even if it was above you, as long as the area was suitable for water. The purpose of water in Feng Shui is to help collect and gather auspicious Qi. If a particular area in a property is identified as an area where the Qi is beneficial, water would be well suited in that sector of the house.

My Hong Kong master always likes to say – don't take things literally. Reading just one sentence from the I-Ching and coming to a conclusion is like staring at the Mona Lisa's hands and deciding that it is not a masterpiece. You need to see the whole picture.

The purpose of WATER in FENG SHUI is to help collect and gather auspicious QI

Plucking a single sentence from the whole volume of the I-Ching and trying to plug it into Feng Shui is irresponsible and can be dangerous at times. One needs to carefully refer to the particular situation in the I-Ching where water above may have been described as being bad. Water above does not necessarily denote disaster or danger.

Now using the 'Secret Art of Common Sense', we can also debunk this little 'Feng Shui Taboo' and I want you to think about this:

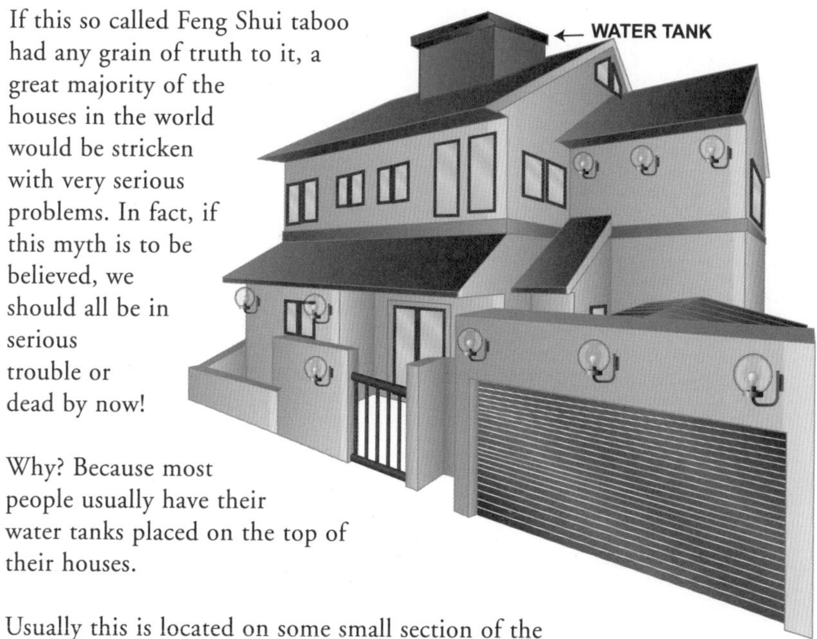

If this so called Feng Shui taboo had any grain of truth to it, a great majority of the houses in the world would be stricken with very serious problems. In fact, if this myth is to be believed, we should all be in serious trouble or dead by now!

Why? Because most people usually have their water tanks placed on the top of their houses.

Usually this is located on some small section of the ceiling, just beneath the roof or at times, in the attic. This is necessary for the operation of the tanks as the gravity ensures a reasonable water pressure. No sensible architects would design a house with the Water Tank UNDER ground.

Let's take it further. If you really do decide to adhere to this taboo...what option do you have left besides removing the tank from your roof? What about people who have jacuzzis and bathtubs located in the upstairs bathrooms. How about sinks in upstairs bathrooms? Are we expected to remove those as well? Besides the heavy cost, you're also going to have problems when it comes to the water pressure in the house's taps.

Water tank located next to a house

There are plenty of people from various walks of life living in homes where the water tank is located on the roof. Are they all doing terribly for themselves? How then can we logically conclude that 'Having Water Above' is a Feng Shui taboo?

Quoting 'raw' theory out of the I-Ching and passing it off as Feng Shui is misguided. The whole context of it must be read and understood before arriving at any theory. Bear in mind that most I-Ching books today are written in the context of divination and not in the perspective of Feng Shui. Many principles need some adjustments before using them as Feng Shui principles.

As I said before, always look at the fundamentals and remember, 'new' fundamentals are not created overnight.

"Plucking a single sentence from the whole volume of the I-Ching and trying to plug it into Feng Shui is irresponsible and can be dangerous at times."

The 'Water on the Right Hand Side of the Main Door' Myth

Many times, in the course of teaching or consulting, I have heard this oft-repeated remark: Water on the right side of the Main Door causes the man of the house to have an affair. The finding of a water feature on the right hand side of their property therefore becomes a major cause for concern.

Now, is this Feng Shui fact or myth?

My first question is: Where did this idea come from? I have searched through many Chinese classical Feng Shui text books for a trace of this 'theory' but found no trace nor mention of it. It seems there is no solid foundation or supporting evidence to this 'theory' in the Feng Shui Classics.

Now, many people claim that this 'theory' is true due to the fact that they've seen several houses with water at the right side of the door and the husband of the house did have an affair.

Well, water on the right, left, back and front can also trigger an affair. In one recent consultation I did, a Period 7 house facing S2 with the Main Door in the South, facing S2 had water on the LEFT. Guess what? The husband was having some fun on the side.

The key to remember here is it's not about WHERE the Water is, but WHAT the Water has triggered. What Qi that is. Certain Flying Stars or Environmental features can cause adultery or extra-marital affairs, not just by the man of the house, but by the lady of the house too. These stars or features do not just exist on the right hand side of a house. They can be in any sector, depending on the landform in the area and the Flying Star chart of the house (and also, the BaZi chart of the resident).

For example, a 4-1 combination in Flying Stars when mildly activated helps promote study or academic prowess. But over-activation, for example by placing excess water, can lead to scandals and adultery.

The real cause of Feng Shui problem is usually over-activation or negative activation of certain bodies of Qi in a house.

Now, perhaps my female readers WOULD like to know, in what instances a husband might stray? (I say 'might' because these circumstances merely indicate a possibility)

In Xuan Kong Feng Shui, a husband (or a wife for that matter!) will stray when certain stars or bodies of Qi are negatively activated. For example, if a particular sector in a house has a 4-1 combination and the man of the house is Kan Gua, and the 4-1 sector sees sharp incoming water (meaning negative water Sha Qi), then it is very likely that he will be embroiled in scandals and affairs. This can be explained by the meanings of the stars. (4-1 with 'negative' water feature denotes scandals and adultery.)

Ordinarily, water on the right side (or the left side for that matter), would not immediately denote that your husband is having and affair.

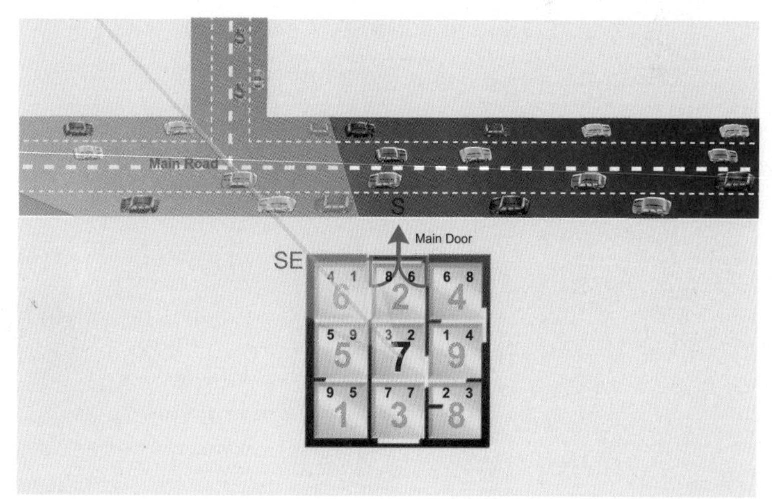

Busy Junction negatively activates the 4-1 combination at the South East sector. A negatively activated 4-1 indicates infidelity, scandals or extra marital affairs.

Now, is this Feng Shui FACT or MYTH?

I hope this helps dispel the myth about Water on the right side of the house. If you do have water on the right side, DON'T WORRY! Find out instead what Flying Stars are activated by that water feature (and do give your husband the benefit of the doubt).

Thus, Water on the right side of the main door causing the man of the house to have an affair seems to be nothing more than a cultural superstition or old wives tale at best.

Apartment No. 14

A woman rang up my office one day and without introducing herself, immediately declared in a disgruntled tone, "I am in number 14".

"Number 14… what?", I asked, after I had ascertained who she was (a seminar attendee of mine). It looks like we Feng Shui practitioners are also expected to be psychic.

She enlightened me – apparently she had been encountering a steady stream of bad luck and she put this down to her apartment unit, which was number 14. In Cantonese, the number '14' sounds like the Cantonese words for 'sure die'.

The Chinese have long held fervent beliefs about the meanings of certain numbers when spoken in Cantonese or in Mandarin, or in any of the other Chinese dialects. In most Asian countries, it's not uncommon to hear people buying houses based on the house number or ensuring that their car number plates have numbers like 1-6-8 or 888.

But while these may 'sound' prosperous or nice (or in the case of the dreaded 4, sound like "die"), numbers really do not carry any Feng Shui effects. I told the lady on the phone that in Chinese (or English for that matter), 14 is 13 + 1 and has nothing to do with "sure die".

"I know, but it sounds like it right?", she insisted.
"Exactly", I pressed my point home, "just because it sounds like it, it doesn't mean that the number of your unit will bring about such an effect. This is just superstition".

Why is it superstition? A number that means one thing in one Chinese dialect may very well mean, or sound like something else in another. So which is a person supposed to believe?

Numbers in Feng Shui calculations are used to represent attributes of Qi – they are not important because they symbolize or sound auspicious. The fact that certain combinations may coincidentally also sound auspicious (such as 6-8 or the 1-6-8 combination or a

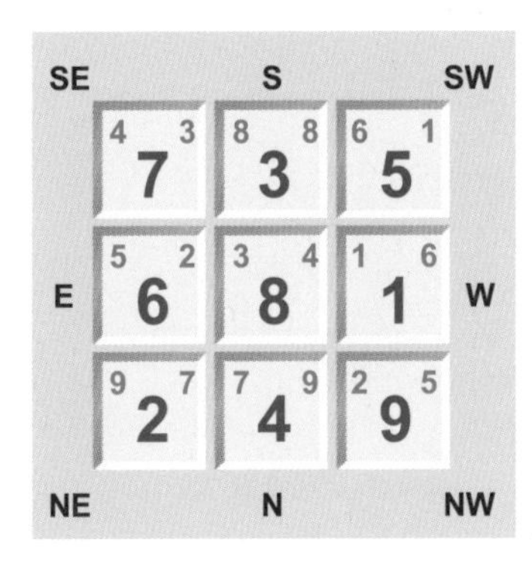

Double 8 Sitting/Facing in Flying Stars), does not mean that they are definitely auspicious or good for luck.

A house with Double 8 Facing or Sitting Structure in Period 8 for example, is not necessarily a more auspicious situation, simply because activating either the Sitting or Facing #8 Star will necessarily entail deactivating the other.

I explained to the lady that the real reason for her troubles was more likely related to the external and internal arrangements within her apartment. I suggested she check the following (and these are quick points that are generally applicable to most properties):

- Check to see if your door is obstructed; Qi should be flowing freely into your unit's Main Door.

- Is your apartment's door facing your favourable directions? Are you tapping into your favourable direction?

- If it is obstructed, narrow and dark, then it is unlikely to invite auspicious QI. It is advisable to rectify this where possible.

- Choose a good room location/sector suitable to your Life Gua and House Gua.

- Sleep in a good direction based on your Life Gua.

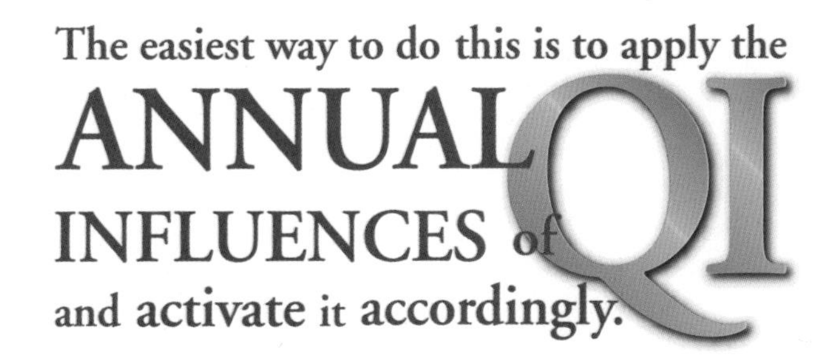

Qi is directional and locational. Occupants need to ascertain the positive and negative locations of Qi within an apartment unit (or house) and tap into them.

The easiest way to do this is to apply the Annual influences of Qi and activate it accordingly. For example, the annual star #8 which is said to influence wealth is in the Northeast sector in 2004. Activate these areas with 'active' objects like a TV, aquarium or something that constantly has activity moves. If you have rooms in these beneficial areas, use them more frequently.

Which floor to purchase an apartment unit in and which unit you intend to purchase within that floor may require that you seek the advice of a Professional Feng Shui Consultant. But remember, the number of your apartment unit bears no significance on the Feng Shui of the unit itself.

Where is My Wealth Sector?

I think the most common question (if not the first question!) any professional Feng Shui practitioner is asked during any Feng Shui audit is: "Where is my Wealth sector?".

Is there really a "wealth" sector in every home?
Yes....and No.

The term 'Wealth Luck' (and Wealth Sector) has been heavily commercialised by pop-feng shui and people tend to have this idea that if they activate their wealth luck or wealth sector, they will become instant millionaires overnight!

In reality, “Wealth Luck” in Feng Shui does not refer to “money falling from the sky” or sudden windfall gains. The actual “luck” a “wealth corner” brings when activated actually refers to beneficial energies that help sharpen the mind, allowing residents to recognize opportunities and helping them perform better in their endeavors.

In Feng Shui terminology, the more appropriate term for ‘Wealth Sector 財位 ’ is the ‘Wang Wei 旺位 ’ or the Prosperous Location. When we say "prosperous" location, we are referring to a location within home where the Qi is strongest and most beneficial. This is because Feng Shui is about harnessing beneficial positive Qi and evading negative Qi in any living environment.

To ascertain the “Wang Wei” location, Feng Shui practitioners use certain methods of calculation depending on which school of Feng Shui they advocate. In the Xuan Kong (Flying Stars) Feng Shui, the Wang Wei is determined by the location of the most prosperous star of the period.

For example, in Period 7 (1984-2003), the most prosperous star (meaning the most prosperous area of Qi) is governed by star number #7. The next best Qi, also known as "Sheng Qi", is governed by Star number #8 as this is the prosperous star for the upcoming Period 8 (2004 – 2023).

A home can be said to have at least two “Cai Wei” or so called “Wealth Sectors”. The task of the Feng Shui practitioner is to locate these corners and activate them correctly to harness the beneficial Qi.

A home can be said to have at least two

"CAI WEI" or so called

"WEALTH SECTORS"

The task of the FENG SHUI practitioner is to locate these corners and activate them correctly to harness the beneficial QI.

財

Now, here is where it gets fun. Qi, like time, is dynamic and cyclical. Every year, the "Wang Qi" shifts from one direction to another. There is a yearly "Wang" (prosperous) sector and a "Shuai" (negative Qi) sector.

In 2003, Prosperous Qi resides in the WEST sector while negative Qi resides in the South East. In 2004, Prosperous Qi is coming in from the North East so it would be ideal to help facilitate this Qi by using a North East direction door, or by using the North East sectors more often.

Your prosperous location is the main 'wealth' sector of the year. While the second best location, as the name implies, is your secondary wealth location of the year.

Year	Prosperous (Wang) Qi Location	Secondary Wealth Sector
2005	South	North
2006	North	South West
2007	South West	East
2008	East	South East
2009	South East	Center
2010	Center	North West
2011	North West	West
2012	West	North East
2013	North East	South
2014	South	North

Contrary to popular misconception, there is no need to place any objects or hang any symbols on the walls to activate the Wealth Luck sectors of the year. Just use this sector (ie: make it your activity room or TV room) more often rather than simply trying to activate it by placing an object there. After all, Feng Shui affects people, not necessarily objects, and logically, by using the room more, it will be more beneficial to the occupants of the house as they are affected by the Wang Qi.

Should it be inconvenient or impossible to use the Prosperous Qi sector or a Prosperous Qi "direction" door, the next best alternative would be to allocate "Yang" or moving objects in that sector for the year. The more activity (Yang energy) you place in the Wang Qi area (the prosperous Qi area), the more you can 'activate' its beneficial energies. Bright lights in this room, for example, will suffice to mildly stimulate the energies in the sector.

Conversely, there is always a sector in the home that is afflicted by negative Qi for the year. This negative energy is borne by the #5 Star and it affects the area that it flies into.

Negative Qi Sectors

Year	Negative (#5 Yellow) Qi
2005	North West
2006	West
2007	North East
2008	South
2009	North
2010	South West
2011	East
2012	South East
2013	Center
2014	North West

'Metal' element of qind chimes help weaken the 'Earth' element of the 5 Yellow Star.

It would be best to use this area as little as possible. The less it is used, the more likely that the negative energies will not affect the occupants of the property.

If you wish, you can further weaken (but not necessarily completely remove) the negative Qi by placing a Metal Wind chime in the negative sector where the #5 Yellow Qi resides. We need to use a Wind Chime made of the Metal element specifically. In the study of the Chinese Five Elements (which is also used in Chinese medical studies), Metal weakens Earth energies. The negative Qi that is coming in from the afflicted direction belongs to Earth and that is why a Metal wind chime helps weaken its strength.

Seeking the Love Corner

I cannot begin to count the number of heartbroken e-mails I get everyday, from all four corners of the Earth, from people professing how desperate they feel and asking how it might be possible to do anything more to 'enhance' their love or relationship corner.

After all, we all want to be loved, if not wealthy! (preferably, both of course) and countless people, attached or otherwise, have spent a considerable amount of wealth trying to 'enhance' this particular nook/cranny of their home.

Often I have to disappoint these people. While there is in fact what can be termed a "Love Corner", this "Love Corner" in fact does not have a fixed location!

Let me explain. There are certain directions and locations in a property that may help its residents foster better relationships. But in Classical Feng Shui, there is no precise location or corner that specifically works to improve your love life.

Unfortunately, we become a society that thrives on the concept of 'instant gratification'. Everything must and needs to happen, right away. We are sold on the idea of quick fixes to nearly every problem we have. From the common cold to divorces - it can be done within 24 hours. So we've come to expect and demand that with the Qi of our environment as well.

For example, many books on Feng Shui today state that the South West location of a house is to be regarded as the universal LOVE corner. Now, the South West sector belongs to the element of Earth (in the cycle of the Five Elements). Somehow, authors and practitioners have managed to rationalise or derive that this is the Love Corner for all individuals and that by enhancing or

placing cures in this corner of the home, you are guaranteed to meet your Knight in Shining Armour (or Rapunzel, whichever takes your fancy).

I understand that this may sound surprising to many of you, but the South West sector is, unfortunately, NOT the universal 'love' sector as popular publicized. We must exercise a little bit of the secret art of common sense. Realistically Feng Shui cannot be so generic!

One may argue that there could be some schools in Feng Shui that would say that the South West IS the love corner and that I should respect these schools. OK, but every 'school' of Feng Shui can trace its unique method of application and formulas to certain age old Classical texts.

I have done the research, asked many Masters and yet cannot find ANY link to this 'new quick-fix' principle of the 'South West' being the universal 'love corner'. There are no ancient records either on this particular 'theory'. So the bottom line questions we as practitioners or researchers of Feng Shui should ask is "what is the basis" for regarding "South West" as the love corner? Why is it the "love" corner? Is it because SouthWest represents the "mother" and mother represents love? If so, then do we mean all the other sectors, which corresponds to the father, son, daughters all does not have love? The trigram "Kun" from the South West does not govern "relationships". So, clearly, it is a very 'new' quick-fix indeed.

Of course some people would say - hey but it works! I've placed some flowers in the South West and I've got a girlfriend! How do you explain that?

In Feng Shui, Qi moves in a cyclical format. Nothing is fixed. Everything is in constant state of flux. Thus every house will have its so called "relationship" corner in different locations depending on the calculation of the internal Qi map of the house, based on its design, layout and immediate environment. Some houses might have a few more of these locations while some, unfortunately, have none. You will just have to check.

And then there are the "Annual" Qi cycles. Every year, certain directional and locational Qi movements in our properties can help us in some romantic endeavors. And if we can locate this, we can tap to it.

Now, in the year 2002, perhaps the South West did have some 'relationship' enhancing capabilities. However, that was because the Annual Flying Star #4 was in that sector. The #4 Green Flying Star has Qi associated with romantic attributes. Tapping into this Qi can help foster better relationships.

In 2003, the Annual Flying Star #3 occupied the South West, indicating breakups or even divorce caused by the negative #3 Flying Star rather than improving love luck. And if you didn't know better and thought that the South West is the 'universal love corner', tapping to this sector of your home in 2003 for 'love' aspects would have resulted in grave consequences.

Feng Shui is a science. There is nothing 'hocus pocus' about Feng Shui. I encourage my students, clients and readers to study it with an inquisitive mind. But every formula must be grounded in logic and explaination. South West being the Universal Love corner just because it is the "Kun" Gua does not qualify as a satisfactory logical answer.

So now, what CAN be done through classical Feng Shui to improve one's relationships?

There are two types of Qi that help foster relationship - the stars #4 and #9. In 2003, the star #4 resides in the East sector. In 2004, you need to look to the South East for the #4 or South for the #9.

To strengthen this effect, if you cannot physically be in the South East or South, try a small water feature. A clear glass vase filled with Water and some plants that grow on Water would be good enough.

The idea of using water is to allow beneficial Qi (in this case, you want the effects of Star #4 or #9) to collect and and benefit you.

Location of the Stars of Romance by year

YEAR	Star #4	Star #9
2004	South East	South
2005	-	North
2006	North West	South West
2007	West	East
2008	North East	South East
2009	South	-
2010	North	North West
2011	South West	West
2012	East	North East

So, to improve relationships in 2004, try using the South East sector instead! You will have better luck with that sector instead of the infamous South West. The annual Qi that could improve relationship matters has shifted to this sector and if you are looking for the 'quick fixes' then the South East is your 'quickest' possible solution.

For a more stable and long lasting solution, you need to evaluate your home and identify areas of which the Qi can help promote and foster better ties and relationship with others in the long run. This evalutation will take into consideration your entire house's internal as well as external conditions.

Feng Shui cannot create a LOVE relationship but it can create opportunities. There is no specific 'love' corner but there are types of 'Qi' that help you build relationships, make you a more pleasant person to be with, make you cheerful and happy - attributes that make you attractive and likable to others!

A Crisis in the Dining Room

An interior designer friend walked dejectedly into my office one afternoon, plopped himself down on my couch and with a huge sigh remarked, "I need some help with Feng Shui, Joey. I have a difficult client who knows a thing or two about Feng Shui and they have me running back to the drawing board each time they stumble across something new. I'm afraid to even propose a new design just in case it goes against their Feng Shui beliefs".

A little information can be a dangerous thing and this client of his had taken some of this information a bit too literally and a bit too far. "Even the mirror in the dining room has become a heated issue" my friend complained.

"Tell me from the beginning" I urged my friend.

Does large miror in the dining room 'double' the food?

It all began when the client insisted that the mirror should reflect the food on the table. It was not a difficult design request and reasonably aesthetically pleasing, so my friend complied.

But then when he showed the client his design, he was informed that the mirror should not cut off the heads or feet of those sitting at the dining table. To top it off, the mirror had to have a bronze frame inscribed with the Chinese character "man" "满 "(meaning 'abundance').

After many sleepless nights and countless re-drawings, the designer somehow managed to incorporate all these requests, only to be told he also had to ensure the mirror didn't reflect the toilet or the road.

This request was simply impossible since the house itself was relatively large and the mirror had to be custom-built to accommodate the large dining wall. There was no way that it would now be able to reflect the food but not anything else.

It seemed the reason for the mirror was the client's wish that the food be 'doubled' when reflected in the mirror. The inscription "man" – to symbolize that they will always have lots of food and never go hungry.

And it might NOT be Meaningful to those who can't read CHINESE!

華文

Here's what I have to say on this whole misguided affair.

If you want to double the food on your dining table, COOK MORE. A reflection in a mirror is merely an illusion; when you finish your food in the real world, you'll find that it's not there in the 'mirrored' world either. This is just an old house-wives tale that mirrors can 'double their food' in the dinning room.

As for the inscription of 'Man' on the frames, that's not going much use either – it is merely a Chinese character that carries the meaning 'abundance'. It's just a Chinese character, nothing more than that. It does not have any magical powers to mysteriously create a lot of 'abundance' just because it means "abundance".

And it might not be meaningful to those who can't read Chinese!

A mirror next to your dining table... good Feng Shui?

I asked my friend and he confirmed that his clients were not Chinese educated. Why not write the word 'abundance' all over the frames? If they can't read Chinese, it might be a good idea to write it in English, right? Whichever language it's written in, it's not going to have any Feng Shui significance.

"I suppose now you'll tell me the dining room table doesn't make much of a difference either", said my designer friend, a resigned expression on his face. "I had to re-design the table that was initially a round glass table. My clients went on and on about how the 'Fire' element in the South sector (where their dining room was), and so there could not be a round table or it would 'counter' the element of their dinning table, because Fire counters Metal".

Now, let's apply the 'Secret Art of Common Sense' to this statement. If this were true, then we all need to have round beds (Metal element) in our bedrooms if the bedrooms are in the North East or South West (since the Earth element of North East or South West would then produce our bed's element 'metal'). Or perhaps we should be sleeping in 'wavy shaped' beds that symbolize Water if we need the 'water element'!

It seems that his clients have perhaps gone overboard and literally taken a religious approach to Feng Shui instead of approaching it from a scientific perspective. This sort of thinking is superstitious and should be discouraged.

A Chinese theme can be a beautiful setting for your home's décor but it really has very little to do with the real Feng Shui. Real Feng Shui is not concerned with interior decoration. Real Feng Shui is to do with the placement and alignment of key features like pathways, walkways, halls, rooms and working areas within your home that allow you to manipulate Qi to your own benefit.

"Well, what then do we need to focus on for the Feng Shui of a dining room?" he asked, hoping I suppose to find some answers he could offer his clients.

Now, the dining room is not regarded as one of the 6 important factors of internal Feng Shui. In the ancient classics, the dining room ranks below the Main Door, Kitchen, Master Bedroom and Living Room. This is because normally residents do not spend considerable amount of time in the dinning room to benefit or be harmed by the Qi in that area.

Generally, the dining room should be located in a spacious and unobstructed area of the home. But there is no need for elaborate, expensive mirrors and paintings as long as the dining room is located where good Qi gathers. As a general rule, the Fu Wei or Yan Nian sectors in a home are suitable areas for a dining room location if you follow BaZhai (8 Mansions). Fu Wei Qi and Yan Nian Qi are often calming and would be ideal for family gatherings and meals. For Flying Star Feng Shui, the dining room may be located where the star combinations 4-1, 4-9, 8-6 or 6-8 are found.

I hope this will go some way towards reducing the punishment and cruelty (in the words of my designer friends) that so many designers are being subjected to these days as their clients become more attuned to Feng Shui.

Remember that Feng Shui is not a religion nor is it a superstitious cultural practice. Feng Shui is also not about making every nook and cranny of our home or office 'oriental' or 'auspicious' looking. The key factor should be 'comfort'. Residents should feel comfortable with the design they have chosen and not be ruled and pressured by superstitions.

The shape of your dining table is not an important factor in a Feng Shui assessment.

It's a Cubicle Thing

I had a call one day from a very nice young gentleman who seemed almost hesitant to tell me what was on his mind. Only after much persuading did he explain that he had read an article about me in a local daily and was contemplating seeking my advice but was afraid that my charges would not be affordable for a wage earner like him. He was concerned over the Feng Shui of his cubicle at work. He couldn't change any of his office's Feng Shui but he was interested to know how he could maximise the Feng Shui of his cubicle.

He briefly explained his cubicle set up and his Feng Shui issues. He felt he lacked support at work, especially since his back was to a window. So, he had placed a tortoise figurine behind him. He was also thinking about sticking a mirror to his PC to 'reflect' some so-called

Sha Qi that he felt was emanating from behind him. You see, as with most offices, the changes he could make to his work area were extremely limited.

I have always believed 'NEVER let what you cannot do interfere with what you CAN do'.

Coming back to the young man in the cubicle - it's a common fallacy that sitting with a glass window behind one's back indicates a less than ideal sitting position. Feng Shui is a study of Qi and how Qi flow affects the residents. If the Qi in your environment is good, you will definitely want it to come in any way it can, including the window.

The only exception to this rule would be when there is a sharp edge from the outside angled at your window behind you, a straight road coming straight at the window, having stagnant or dirty water just outside the window or nearby and if there are other negative Feng Shui structures in the vicinity of the window.

"But I was under the impression that the glass at the back will leave my back exposed and bad energies will affect me?" insisted the young man.

My point exactly. IF there are negative energies, yes they may affect you but if there are none and you instead have positive energies, why would you not want these to come in (from the window) and influence the Qi in your cubicle?

My next suggestion to him was to not bother about the mirror. Mirrors are not considered a primary Feng Shui cure. If there is negative Qi coming from the glass window, the mirror will have nothing more than a negligible effect on it. A better, and often more effective idea is to simply keep the blinds of that window closed.

Many people often overlook one very simple point: Are you facing your favorable directions? Favorable directions help heighten your work performance. If you're already tapping into one of your good directions, then the glass behind your back should be no great cause for concern.

Personal action is possibly the most Effective and Practical answer when it comes to Feng Shui 'CURES'.

Apply this quick system of points to gain some perspective on this matter. If you are facing your best direction (Sheng Qi), your Feng Shui point score is 100 points. Let's say having a window behind you now causes you to lose (at most!) 20 points - you're still ahead by a luxurious 80 points!

Not bad at all is it?

At times, fear can do more harm than anything else. It often places a mental restriction on a person and causes them to perform a lot less better than they really can. In 8 out of 10 cases that I have seen, it's psychological hurdles that hold back many people and not their Feng Shui.

Here are a few useful guidelines that can be applied for Cubicle Office Feng Shui:

- If you are familiar with Xuan Kong (Flying Star) Feng Shui, and you have an opportunity, find a location in your office that supports your work. This need not necessarily mean hogging the area where the Facing or Sitting star #8 is located (although that is a good idea), you can just as well tap into the energies of the 4-1 combination if you are in marketing to keep you in peak performance. You can also tap combinations like #1-#6 for professions related to managing, engineering and administration. Each combination in Xuan Kong can serve a particular job function.

- Selecting a suitable, favorable facing direction while working is yet another important and effective method for cubicle Feng Shui. If you're a little uncertain about this, use the Eight Mansions Calculator at **www.masteryacademy.com** to find out your Best Direction or Sheng Qi.

- Finally, take note of the annual and monthly influences of Qi and take the necessary precautions (or capitalize upon opportunities where possible). By far, this is the best advice I can give you – know what's coming and be prepared for it. Much of Feng Shui does not always depend on a physical object or item as 'cure' but rather the person's personal actions and deeds.

For example, assume the #3 star flies into your cubicle for the month. You then already know that arguments, misunderstandings and disagreements are bound to crop up. So what should you do? Moving out is an option, or you can always try some quick re-decorating using the color red to weaken the #3 star, but if neither of this is an option, then simply practice self control. Take note of your actions and attitudes and even if the Qi makes you a little cranky this month, a little restraint will go a long way towards ensuring harmony between your colleagues. Personal action is possibly the most effective and practical answer when it comes to Feng Shui 'cures'.

There's no substitute for hard, smart work and a positive attitude when it comes to climbing the career ladder. But combine all this with good Feng Shui and you'll improve your chances for a meteoric rise to the top.

'NEVER let what you cannot do interfere with what you CAN do'.

Bedroom Ecstasy

We spend one third of our lives in the bedroom – understandably, the bedroom is therefore one of the key areas to be examined in any Feng Shui consultation and often the subject of requests for tips or taboos from students and enthusiasts. So, what are the taboos for the bedroom? What should a person do or not do within the scope of their bedroom?

One of the most important steps in understanding Feng Shui applications for 'bedrooms' is to first determine the Yin and Yang nature of the 'function' of a bedroom. Feng Shui is a study of Yin and Yang. Generally we say the external is Yang and the internal is Yin. Inside a house, the doors, pathways and living areas are 'Yang' and the bedrooms are 'Yin'. Yang Qi is associated with activeness and accomplishments. Yin Qi is passive and is associated with our health, our mental state and general well-being. Now don't get me wrong, Yin Qi here does not mean anything 'negative'. Yin Qi here merely refers to the subtle and gentle nature, the passive nature of Qi.

A bedroom should not be too 'Yang'

The idea of bedroom Feng Shui is to have tranquility and 'Yin' Qi flowing smoothly. If a room is overly Yang, this defeats the basic nature of bedroom Feng Shui. What do I mean by overly Yang? For instance, if the bedroom has too many windows or more than one entrance to the bedroom, this creates flow of 'active' Qi and this throws off the balance of Yin and Yang. When the Qi is unstable, the bedroom has 'bad' Feng Shui. It's really that simple.

There are two aspects of Feng Shui that we need to assess when analyzing the Feng Shui of a bedroom. The first being the typical formulae-based assessment to determine the type of Qi affecting the room. The other aspect of bedroom Feng Shui is the room layout and placement of the door, bed and window. But let me first talk on some of the common questions (and misconceptions) that there are out there about bathrooms.

"Is water in the bedroom a bad thing?" is one of the questions I get all the time, when on the topic of bedroom Feng Shui. Water in the bedroom apparently will cause a couple to argue or lead to relationship problems.

The answer to this question is yes and no. If water is not condusive to the room, a negative influence most certainly will be felt. For example, if a room has negative Facing Stars (according to Flying Star Feng Shui), water is only going to bring about a disastrous consequences. On the other hand, if water is placed correctly and the room is suited for it, then there's really nothing to worry about. Only in exceptional cases, where the room has Peach-Blossom stars, can having water in that room lead to relationship troubles.

A glass of water next to your bed. Should you be worried?

If the water is still and it is not in very large quantity, it's usually nothing to worry about. Otherwise, everyone who keeps a glass of water on the nightstand for a midnight drink will wake up in the morning and finds their wealth (or spouse) are gone!

Another frequently asked question is whether flowers in a bedroom will create too much Yang energy. Flowers are neither Yang nor Yin Qi and they do not create anymore Qi in your room than there already is. As long as you are not allergic to them, go right ahead and have them in your bedroom!

I am occasionally also asked if en-suite bathrooms might be somehow 'undesirable' for bedrooms by creating Yin Qi in the bedroom and suppressing good luck.

Now, let's face the facts here – en-suite toilets are a great convenience and pose no health hazards unless something is blocked somewhere. This is in complete contrast to the olden days, when toilets usually comprised a hole in the ground or a bucket which had to be emptied. Toilets back then were usually foul smelling places and a breeding ground for diseases. My question therefore is: where is the Yin Qi? In any case, the en-suite toilet occupies a miniscule area of your home in which you probably spend a grand total of 45-60 minutes a day. So, there is nothing to worry about - an en-suite toilet is not emitting any negative Feng Shui so long as you keep it clean and pleasant smelling.

Now, what are the key aspects of bedroom Feng Shui that you OUGHT to be looking at?

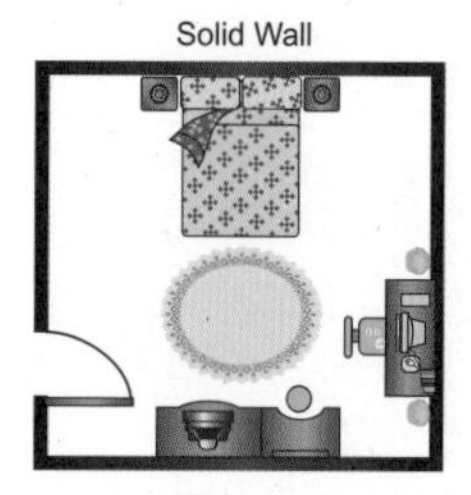

- The most important thing in your bedroom is quite obviously the bed. As far as possible, locate your bed against a solid wall, align your headboard to your favorable direction and locate your bed in a sector where there are good mountain stars.

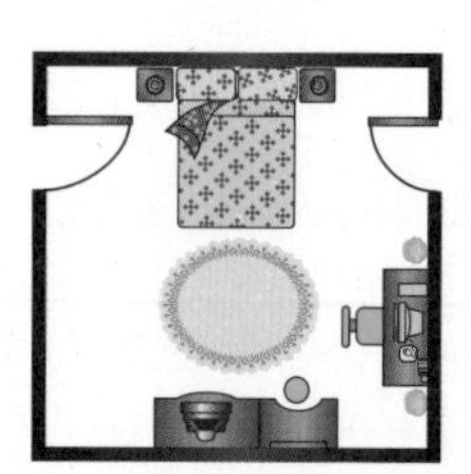

Bed located between two doors. Bad Feng Shui.

- An often overlooked factor in a person's bedroom is the bedroom door. Even with a room in a good sector of your home, try and ensure that the door faces your favorable direction or at least located in a favorable 'location' of the room. In this way, you are geared to receive the positive Qi that this additional factor bestows.

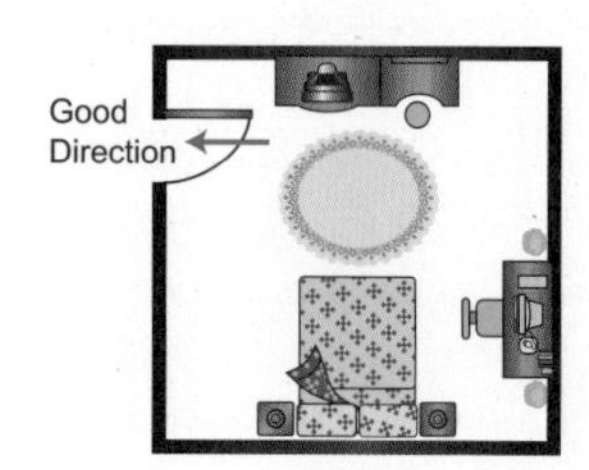

A Fishy Story

It's not often that I get urgent calls from clients literally screaming for help them but that was what happened recently. A very agitated Mrs Chan just had one of her fishes go belly up on her.

She was distraught but not because the fish had died. Instead, it was because she had heard somewhere that when her pet goldfish dies, it has 'sacrificed' its life to protect Mrs Chan's. "Thank goodness the goldfish absorbed the bad luck meant for me," she wailed over the phone. She now wanted to know what was in store for her.

I calmed Mrs Chan down and reassured her that there were no terrible accidents or falling comets headed her way. Only then did I manage to get a word in and let her know in no uncertain terms that her poor goldfish HAD NOT committed a sacrificial act to save her life.

Needless to say, Mrs Chan was a bit disappointed with my answer.

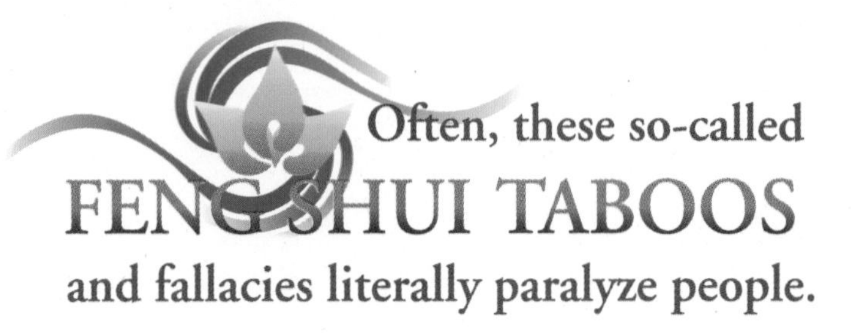

"I thought you were a Feng Shui expert? How can this also you don't know?", she said, almost skeptically. "I've read in a few Feng Shui books that say it's good when a fish you keep dies because it has sacrificed its life to absorb the evil effects or negative energies meant for the owner."

Now I love a challenge. And Mrs. Chan's little experience is just the kind of challenge I like to tackle.

This notion of the 'sacrificial fish' is nothing more than an old wives tale. Of course I have heard about it, but fact of the matter is, this has nothing to do with Feng Shui. It is pure superstition, plain and simple. A fish is just a fish. Its main preoccupation is to swim around in your fish tank and provide some entertainment or joy to you as a pet. It doesn't have any special, magical powers and it in no way it's going to 'absorb' your bad luck.

It is the element or polarity of 'water' that we want to use when an aquarium is prescribed in a Feng Shui consultation. Water is Yang and active energy - even when it's still, water particles are constantly moving. We use water to harness the Qi in the environment or home. The fishes in the tank merely keep the water lively and active; other than this, they serve no real Feng Shui purpose.

Kuo Po (believed to be the ancient founding father of Feng Shui) himself, in the very basic theory of Feng Shui, wrote that "Qi is dispersed by the wind and gathers by the boundaries of water." Water has this ability to allow Qi to collect and settle. Which is why a good practitioner will recommend that his/her client position an aquarium or pond in the section of the house where good Qi resides.

The crucial point to be concerned about is the LOCATION of the water or aquarium. It has nothing to do with your fishes, regardless of what types of fishes you keep (again another fallacy is that Kois or Arowanas bring you abundant wealth). Feng Shui is not about having your pets 'sacrifice' themselves like lemmings leaping into water. If you are planning on having an aquarium, make sure the water is clean and healthy for your fishes.

I recommended that Mrs Chan check the water in her tank or maybe get an expert to see if the fish had some sort of skin disease. I also suggested that she should perhaps get the water cleaned more often and the filter changed.

My short Feng Shui lesson over the phone seemed to calm down Mrs. Chan who finally understood the superstition behind the dead fish and felt better by the end of our conversation. So, the next time you hear a friend proudly declare just how noble their now-dead fish was, tell them this story and remember, there's a difference between true, classical Feng Shui and popular Chinese superstition.

The Water Fish Blues

Of late, I have been getting a number of questions from clients and students about, of all things, the Flower Horn Fish. All of them seem to have only one question on their mind – is this the ULTIMATE 'Feng Shui fish' for Period 8? A magical fish capable with extremely powerful Feng Shui powers?

According to a breeder friend of mine, the Flower Horn fish, also known as Hua Luo Han, is a product of cross breeding of cichlids which results in the

protruding lump on the forehead. It's an aggressive fish with bright colours and some patterns which seem to resemble numbers or Chinese characters on its body. I don't know how or where this got started but nearly every aquarium and pet store is now on the bandwagon – the Feng Shui Fish for your Feng Shui-ed home.

Even some usually practical students have begun to draw their own conclusions and new theories as to WHY this is a Feng Shui Fish. Just that day, one student explained the hypothesis to me.

He said that the Flower Horn was a Period 8 fish because Period 8 is represented by the Gua Gen or the Mountain and the Flower Horn supposedly has a lump on its head that looks like a mountain! (I am afraid to ask what we Feng Shui practitioners are now supposed to make of cows, goats and other farm animals that also have prominent looking 'mountains' on their heads – will they join the list of Period 8 mascots?)

In Period 7, the Arowana was the Feng Shui fish for the period as it looked like a 'Shining Blade' and Period 7 was governed by the Dui Gua which is the element of Metal, explained my enthusiastic student.

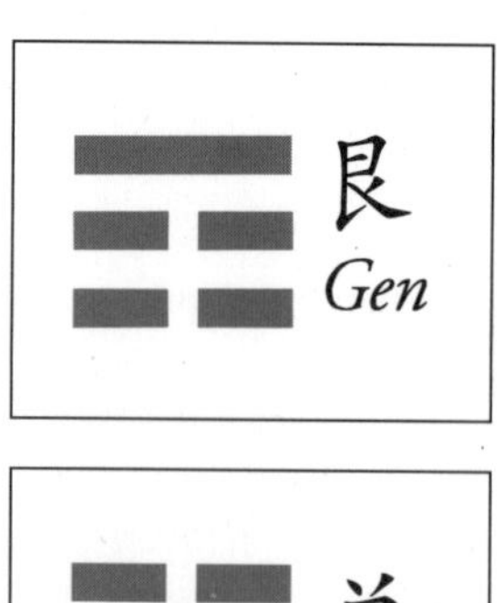

He appeared to have derived his theory from the Flying Star Feng Shui Gua attributes. My student happily acknowledged this.

"Yeah, I sort of figured it out one day when I was studying the Flying Star numbers – they seem to relate to the trigrams a lot. So, I figured the elements and symbols of the Gua played an important role and it suddenly dawned to me that this is why the fishes (Arowana and Flower Horn) are so popular".

I probed into this hypothesis a bit more, "Which classics did you derive this theory from?". He was quiet for a while and then he said he didn't know if there were any classics relating to Flying Star Feng Shui and fish.

The Arowana.
A Feng Shui Fish?

So, then I asked him, "You say the Arowana is a Period 7 fish, so obviously it's not going to be much help in Period 8. Will you be flushing the poor thing down the drain now that it has supposedly outlived its usefulness?". (Arowanas are also very expensive fish and can fetch a princely sums for larger very special varieties.)

Let's set the record straight. There is NO such thing as a Feng Shui fish. If it swims like a fish, has fins like a fish and can breathe in water like a fish – it's a fish.

A fish is definitely an attractive feature in the aquarium but I must point out that any reference it may have to wealth is only SYMBOLIC and has no Feng Shui value to it. Feng Shui is not about symbols. It is about real Qi. A Flower Horn fish is not going to be emanating any Qi from its body. Furthermore, how can a fish, grown by aquatic breeders, make you money?! Unless you're an active competitor in Fish contests and win because of your beautiful Flower Horn fish, there is no way it's going to be bringing you abundant wealth.

Whatever symbols you may be able to see on the fish's body are merely its own marking and do not indicate any special Feng Shui powers.

"But the rich guys SWEAR by it", my student insisted. "If they're already rich, they can afford to spend the $10,000 for the fish and not feel it. Rather than adding to their wealth, it more likely massages their egos," I explained to my student.

All this about the Flower Horn fish being the ultimate Feng Shui fish comes from a wholly incorrect notion that 'water' brings wealth or another popular notion that fish bring money luck.

Water helps activate the Qi in that particular area of the house and this helps you perform better and more readily take advantage of opportunities that present themselves. The fish are there to keep the water active and moving. On their own, they do nothing to make you money! Keep in mind that it is the location of the aquarium that helps promote Qi in the house. If your aquarium is placed in the correct area of your home, then any fish will suffice.

Don't get me wrong, I am not saying that you should not be collecting Flower Horns. They are attractive fishes that fetch a high price and people are naturally inclined to keep them. But in no way should it be regarded as a Feng Shui fish or having Feng Shui powers.

Say Something Nice

A frantic newly-wed bride called me one morning, sounding very distressed and concerned. I was a bit surprised to receive an SOS so soon from her – I had done a BaZi analysis for her and her fiancé and also selected their wedding date. As I had recalled, the wedding had been a festive celebration, with all the bells and whistles.

Gong Xi Fa Cai

It turned out that her concerns stemmed from the failure of the 'Tai Kam Che' (usually a woman who leads the couple through the wedding traditions and serves as a Master of Ceremonies) to wish the couple with the tradition greeting of 'living together happily ever after in nuptial bliss'.

It is a Chinese tradition that one should greet another person with auspicious sayings during any festival or family occasion. All the more so during celebrations like weddings and the Chinese New Year. The newly-wed bride naturally was concerned that her and her husband's future together and their matrimonial happiness would be plagued by this oversight. "My marriage feng shui is all ruined!" she wailed over the phone and wanted to know what she could do about the situation.

"Nothing" I replied. "you don't have to do anything." She was quite surprised by this answer. 'Did your husband greet you with a good morning today?' I asked. "Err...not that I can remember," she replied a little puzzled. "And was today a particularly bad day for you because of this?" I inquired further. "Of course not lah!", she replied.

That is the answer right there, dear readers.

Auspicious sayings and traditional greetings have been a part of Chinese culture for as long as many of us can remember. There are auspicious sayings and greetings for almost any Chinese celebration or event. This naturally gives rise to the question: just how auspicious are these auspicious sayings and greetings and do they really have any effect on real life?

'*Fu*' Luck

'*Lu*' Prosperity

'*Shou*' Longevity

Whereas once, displaying **Chinese Calligraphy** was like displaying art in one's home, **today,** **Chinese Calligraphy** has been attributed with

FENG SHUI POWERS!

Traditional auspicious sayings and greetings during festive seasons or ceremonies such as weddings are nothing more than 'feel good positive affirmations'. There's nothing 'Feng Shui' about them. After all, no one has a miserable Christmas if nobody wishes him or her 'Merry Christmas'. And certainly, many of us have received our fair share of 'Gong Xi Fa Cai' (Wishing You Great Prosperity) greetings over the years – are we all millionaires? Obviously not.

Likewise with Chinese calligraphy. Whereas once, displaying Chinese calligraphy was like displaying art in one's home, today, Chinese calligraphy has been attributed with Feng Shui powers! As if having the word 'Fu' hanging on your wall will help you grow wealth or placing the characters 'Double Happiness' on your walls will magically help induce romance.

This is not Feng Shui in any sense but rather wishful thinking!

'*Xi*' Double Happiness

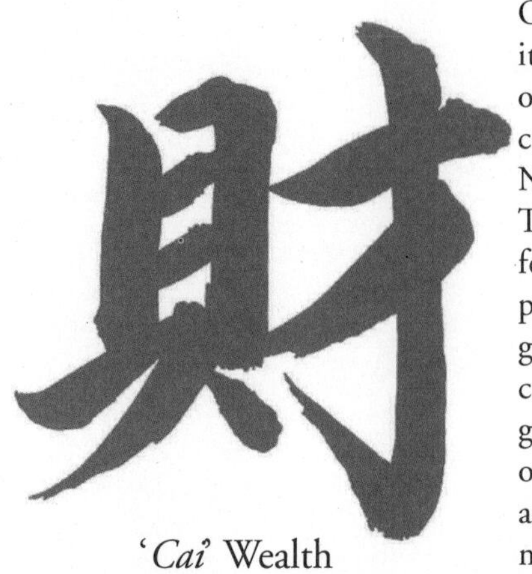

‘*Cai*’ Wealth

Of course, there's nothing wrong in itself with offering auspicious greetings or traditional greetings during celebrations like weddings, the Lunar New Year or on an everyday basis. These provide a certain cheer and festivity to celebrations and no doubt, a positive start to the day is always a good way to start it! Equally, Chinese calligraphy or illustrations of auspicious greetings or sayings add a certain oriental touch to a home or an office and can, in certain times, provide much needed inspiration or motivation.

But other than a psychological uplift, auspicious greetings and sayings or Chinese calligraphy have no Feng Shui connotations or Feng Shui powers as they were. Remember, as with all superstitions, taboos and traditional practices, it's wise to always practice a little COMMON SENSE.

The Best Kept Feng Shui Secret

Feng Shui as you all know, has a bit of a reputation for being a mythical, mysterious, almost magical art. You know how it is – put this here and boom, you're a millionaire. Activate Peach Blossom and you'll have boyfriends or girlfriends by the dozen soon. A Fishtank in your house brings wealth – who doesn't know that one?

And of course, every Feng Shui practitioner has a secret formula or formulae, passed to them by their masters and teachers, which promise to unlock incredible wealth (wealth after all, seems to be the only reason for Feng Shui these days).

I'm going to share with you an extremely profound Feng Shui secret and it's called the 'Secret Art of Common Sense'.

Generally, there is absolutely no reason why it is Bad Feng Shui just because there is Water above the rooms.

In the course of my teaching and the numerous emails I receive daily from people and students all over the world, I have been asked many questions about Feng Shui and the various theories, principles and myths that surround it. Half of these questions can honestly be answered with a little common sense.

Let me give you a few examples. I am often asked if it is wrong or bad Feng Shui for a home to have rooms under water (for example, having a swimming pool on the roof). Generally, there's absolutely no reason why it is bad Feng Shui just because there is water above the rooms. Common sense would tell you that if this was really true, every hotel would be bankrupt by now (since by necessity, every room has a bathroom that is ABOVE another room).

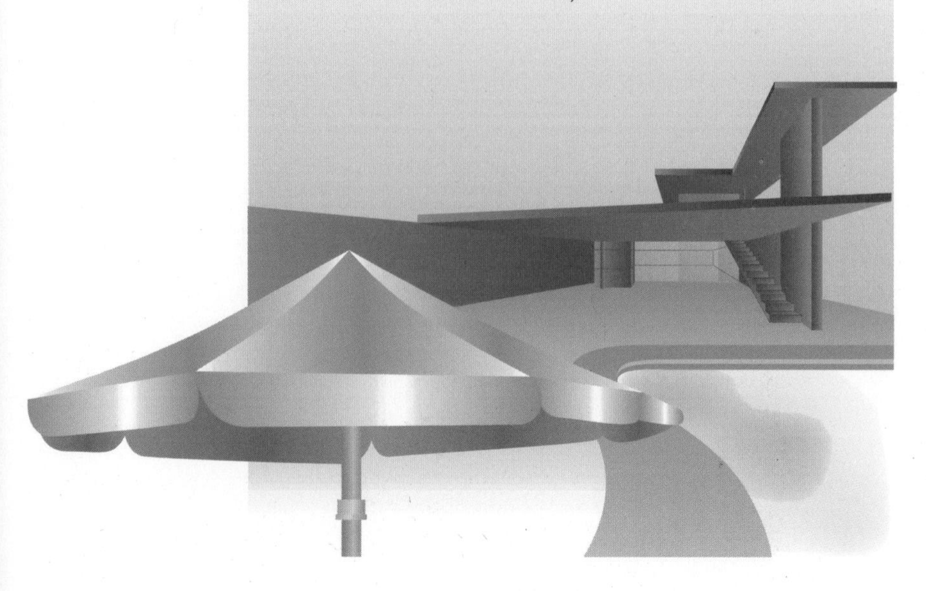

Let's take it one step further: if this taboo was actually true, this would mean that houses could not have toilets or bathrooms on the 2nd floor and we would all have to place our water tanks underground (something which we all know, does not happen).

Another question I often get is about toilets – are toilets considered negative Qi or is it bad Feng Shui to have a toilet located in an area of the house with good Qi.

Again, using common sense – in order to be affected by the Qi, a person has to spend a considerable amount of time in the area. Hence, when evaluating the Internal Factors of the house, practitioners always look at the Main Door, the Bedrooms and the Kitchen. These are areas we spend a lot of time in or utilise a lot. How much time can one person spend in the toilet? At the most, 1 hour a day!

Let's take it further – assuming that toilets are negative Qi or should be located in negative areas of Qi in a home, what are we to do then when faced with a large house with up to 20 toilets? Are they all to be located in one area?

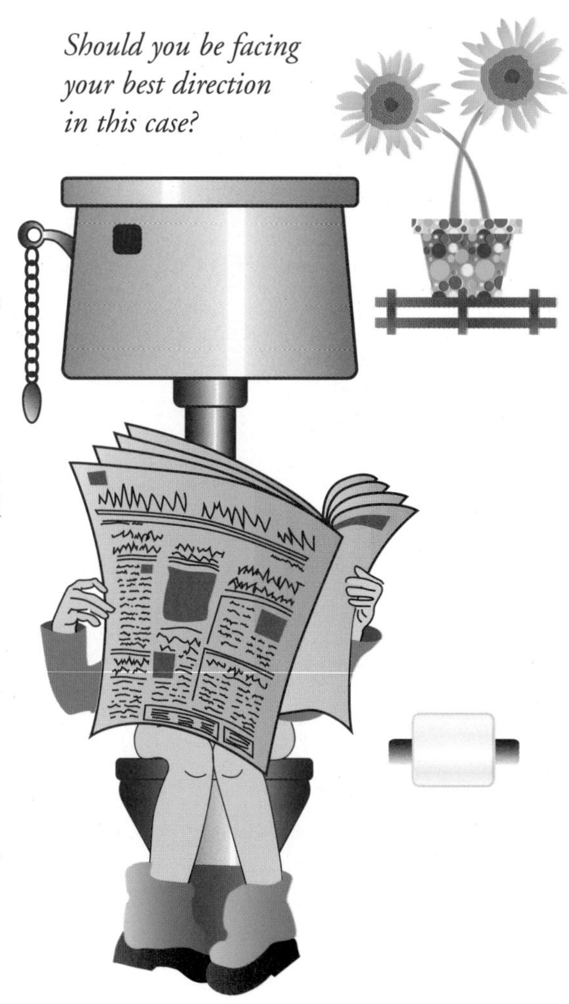

There is nothing mysterious, mythical or magical about Feng Shui. It is a science that is grounded in proper theory and principles, all which can be logically explained. And like any area of study, a little common sense goes a long long way!

Arousing the Dragon!

I don't think there's a term that's more publicized in Feng Shui than 'Dragon'. It's practically a catchphrase amongst Feng Shui practitioners and students. What's the fascination with Dragons?

The most basic and fundamental principle in Feng Shui is 'Seek the Dragon'. This of course raises more questions: What exactly does this mean – to Seek the Dragon? And what really is a Dragon?

If a picture of a fire-breathing, scaly creature found in the medieval days springs to mind, banish the thought! In Feng Shui, Dragons are a reference to the following:

- Mountains
- Water ways
- Sitting Stars
- Facing Stars
- Pathways
- Mountain ranges

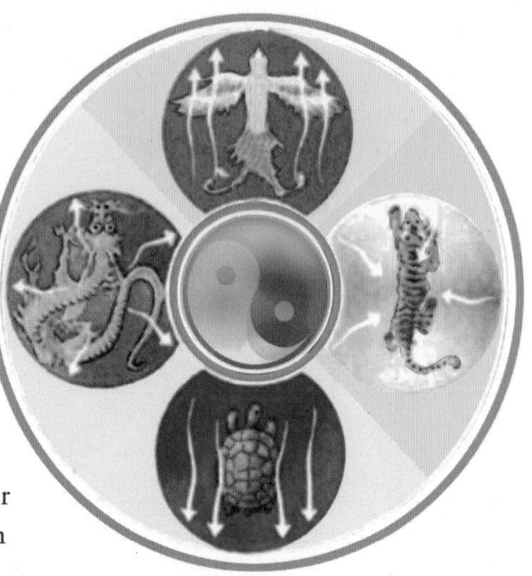

Ancient Chinese philosophers used the term loosely to mean or refer to many different things, which has created a problem for those of us studying it in today's environment.

When examining the topic of Dragons, we need to refer to a number of very old and ancient classics on the subject. The three more popular ones are: The Burial Book (Zhang Jing), The Yellow Emperor's Mansion Classics (Huang Di Zhai Jing), and Snow Heart Classics (Xue Xin Fu). This is not an exhaustive list; for simplicity, I've just chosen the ones that are more frequently referred to.

If you've had a chance to go through these classics, you will note that although these books seem to refer to the same thing when speaking about dragon formations, upon further analysis their approach almost seems contradictory! This perhaps explains why there are so many different schools of thought on this subject.

The term 'Dragon' itself is quoted as such in the following classics:

Kuo Pu in the Burial Book said: *"Earth has Four Formations, Qi comes from Eight Directions."*

The Four Formations he was referring to are "Left Green Dragon, Right White Tiger, Front Red Phoenix and Back Black Tortoise".

In the Yellow Emperor Mansions Classics it is stated:

"Yang House, it is auspicious for Yang Qi to overcome Yin Qi."
"Yin House, it is auspicious to have Yin Qi overcome Yang Qi."
"The Yin and Yang Qi is the Dragon."

Whereas in the Snow Heart Classics, there is a line that says:

"The Dragon is the mountain's movement, ranges. Moves up and down, turns and bends, transforms and undulates like a Dragon. Thus it is called a Dragon."

When we read these lines, it appears that the 'Dragon' means different things in different contexts in the classics. The question that lingers is, are they all referring to the same thing?

De-mystifying the Dragon

There are three significant perspectives of DRAGONS in Classical Feng Shui.

Almost every student or enthusiast of Feng Shui knows about or has heard about the famous "Left Green Dragon", "Right White Tiger", "Front Red Phoenix" and "Back Black Tortoise" principle. These are known as the Four Celestial Animals. So what does this particular Dragon refer to?

Dragon Veins

The 'Green Dragon' that this concept refers to is a symbolic representation of the Left Sha. If you are not clear on what 'Sha' is, it's actually the embracing ranges to a property. (see image below)

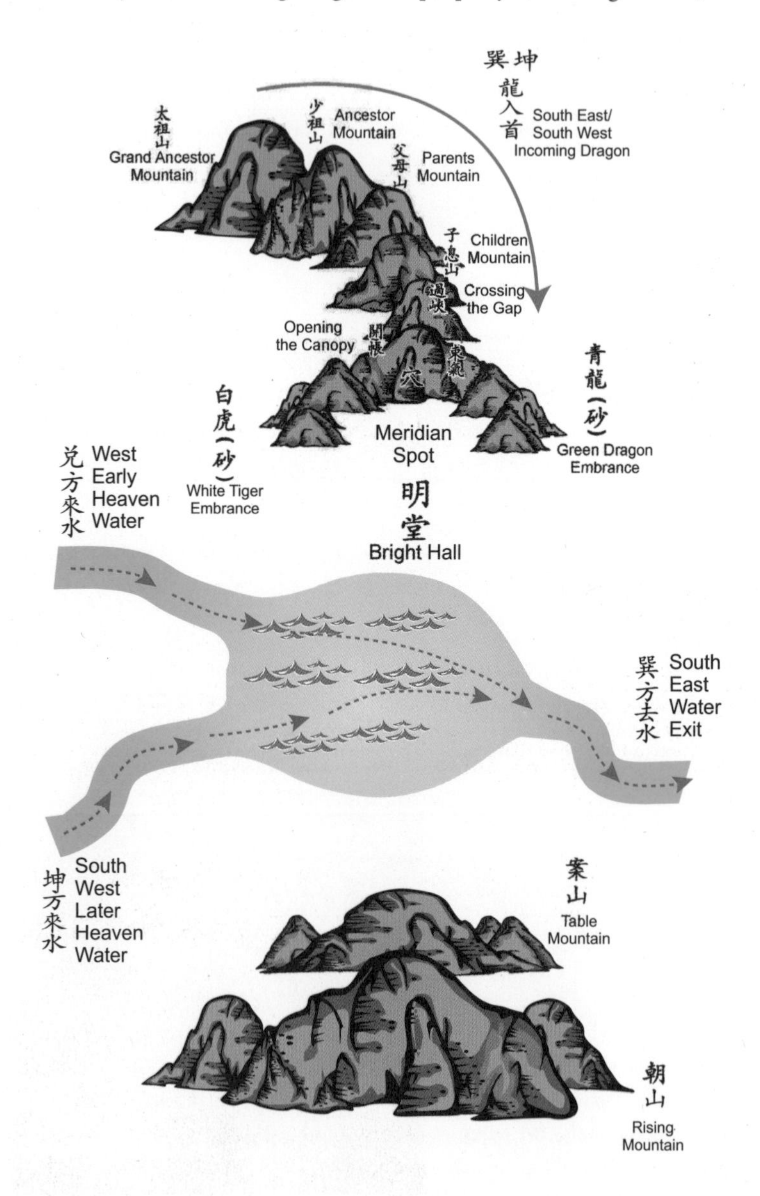

Basic Dragon-Vein assesment using the Dragon Gate Eight Formations method.

Hence, when someone speaks of the Green Dragon with reference to your property, it basically means the mountain ranges on the left hand side of the property embracing it.

In the Yellow Emperor Classics, there is the mention of the 'Qi Dragon'. What does this particular Dragon mean then? 'Qi Dragon' is actually in reference to the Qi that is formed within the structure and formation of a house. It may also be called the Dragon of the House but it does not refer to a physical mountain; instead it's a reference to the body of Qi within your home.

Dragon Embrace

The traditional reference to the Dragon is found in the Snow Heart Classics (Xue Xin Fu) – it is from this Classic that we derive the reference to undulating mountain ranges, the movement of mountains as 'dragons'. The Dragons or mountains are carriers of Qi and are referred to as Qi Mai or Qi Veins.

Certain modern Feng Shui enthusiasts might call thus 'dragon symbology' and equate pictures and figurines of dragons with this natural dragon phenomenon. However, I feel this takes the concept a little too far and out of context. Remember, the term 'Dragon' is used synonymously to describe patterns, formations and movements of Mountains. It can also be used to label types of Qi in a house.

Once a Dragon is sighted, the next move is to seek the Dragon's Lair or Dragon Spot, known as "Chen Lung Zi Shu". Feng Shui practitioners look to find the location where the 'Dragon's Main Qi' converges. When this 'spot' has been located, using proper directioning and positioning, a practitioner will then attempt to tap into this Qi in order to benefit from it. This was the goal of authentic traditional Feng Shui in the old days.

The theory may be relatively easy to understand in a class, but the physical process of 'locating the Dragon Spot' or 'Chasing the Dragon's Vein' is truly a hands-on experience that cannot be replicated in a classroom. It is rare for today's students of Feng Shui to have an opportunity to walk the mountains – an essential aspect of completing their educational path in Feng Shui.

Traditional Xuan Kong has always been focused on locating the Dragon Spot, but most people today are only aware of Flying Stars and 8 Mansions hence the lack of awareness about the Dragon Spot. Flying Stars and 8 Mansion are considered newer systems of Feng Shui, by the way.

A key function of a Feng Shui master is to ascertain the quality of the 'dragons' and of course, how to 'arouse' or to tap into its potential. Hence, the phrase *the art of 'arousing the dragon'!*

The Chicken Out of the Bag

One day, I ran into an old school friend whom I hadn't seen in a while. I was busy travelling and he was pre-occupied with his fledgling business. So we took the opportunity to catch up.

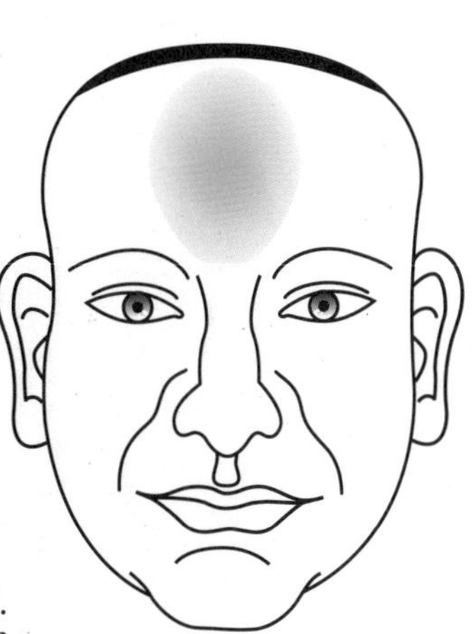

Green Qi at the Cardinal Points

As we were chatting, I caught a glimpse of a greenish patch of Qi on his forehead (I study and practice Face Reading or Mian Xiang). This area encompasses what we refer to in Face Reading as one of the '13 Cardinal Points'. Green Qi on the forehead in the month of the Ox denotes the occurrence of a frightening event.

I asked him if he had been involved in any accidents recently but he said no. I probed a bit further, not satisfied with his answer and to be honest, curious as to what might have caused this phenomenon.

After a few more questions, I discovered one incident that should have held no great significance but did in this case. His house had caught fire recently but fortunately, it did not cause any real damage beyond a chicken in the oven that ended up being heavily over-cooked (burnt to a crisp actually).

My curiosity got the better of me and with my friend's agreement, I went to take a look at his home that same afternoon. I measured his house's Facing and found that it faced Xun, (SE2) and sat on Qian (NW2). It was an old house, built in the 1960's from what I could ascertain but as his family had moved in only in 1985, I used a Period 7 chart. I immediately recognised this as a Pearl String Formation.

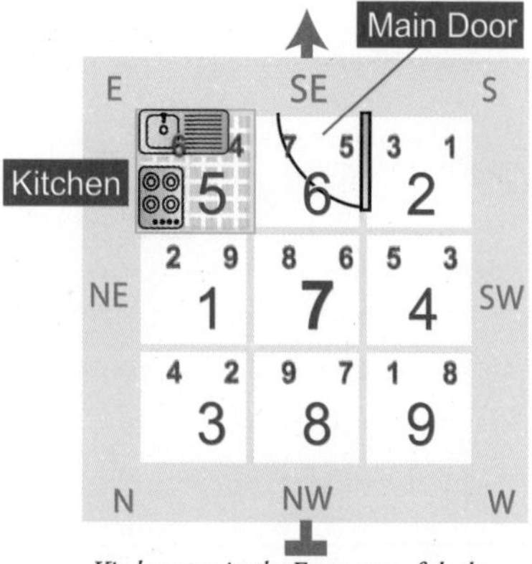

Kitchen was in the East sector of the house

Unfortunately for my friend, the structure was not supported closely by the environment. His main door opened in the Xun (SE) palace but the kitchen, our main area of interest, was in the Zhen (East) palace. Using small Tai-Ji, I ascertained that the stove was located in the North East

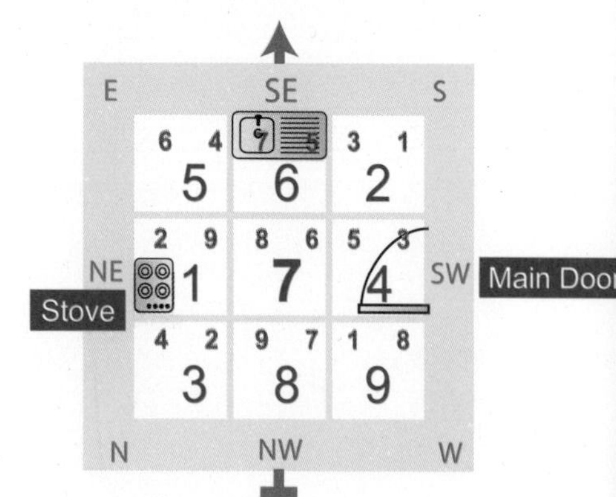

Small Taiji Chart of the Kitchen

sector of the kitchen. The door to the kitchen was in the Kun palace. The small fire incident took place in January 2003.

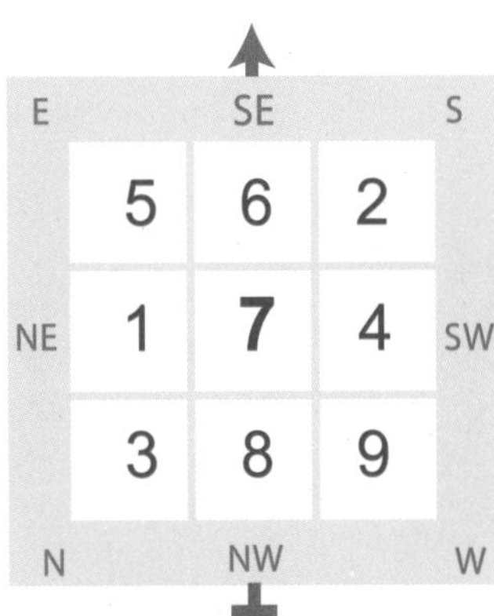

2002 Flying Star Chart

It was a novel bit of analysis that I couldn't resist undertaking.

My friend himself is a Gua 2 but his mum (who does all the cooking in the house) is a Gua 9. In January 2003, the Monthly #5 was located at their main door, with the monthly #4 flying into the kitchen.

The kitchen's Zhen palace has the original combination of the 6-5-4 stars. In 2003, which was the year of Ren Wu 壬午, it was visited by the destructive #5 Yellow Star. It would leave this sector after February 4th 2003 but with the year ending, the energies of the incoming #4 Wood Qi were becoming more prevalent.

Montly Star Chart for January 2003

The stove was placed on the small Tai-Ji of stars 2-9 with a base star of #1. For a 'fire' to start, there must be 'seeds' or a source to the fire – so what was the fire starter?

The culprit was the 'Wood' element. The source of Wood in this case was the monthly star #4 in the East palace with the #3 monthly star in the Kun palace.

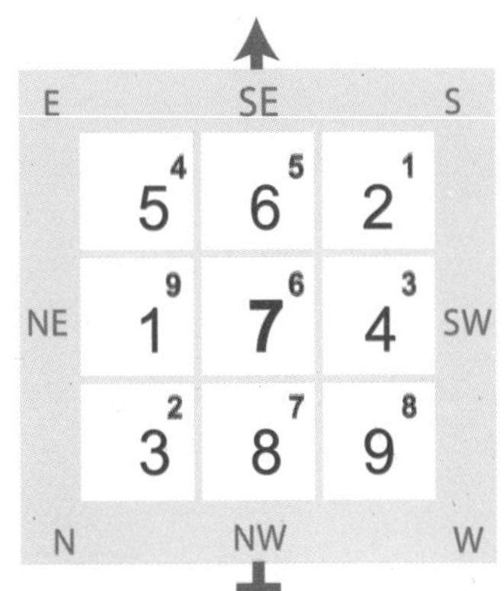

January 2003 Year + Monthly Star Chart

The monthly #9 star is in the North East and Kun represents Mother, as well as the Gua #2 person. So, the fire inadvertently occurred because of the Mother (who is Gua 9) who had a son with a Gua 2. The #4 star also represents, among many other things, chicken. Hence, the unedible chicken caused by the small fire.

Many ancient Chinese texts say that a Wood-Fire combination, like 3-9 and 4-9 combinations, produce smart children. This is true in a sense. In BaZi (Four Pillar), this is called the 'Wood Fire Brilliance' combination. The olden scripts also go on to say that fire can be started with a 2-7 and 9-7 combination.

However, this is a rather simple analysis of combinations. There must of course be an element of wood for any fire to start but the wood must be a suitable 'type' of wood.

In my friend's case, the #5 Yellow Star does contribute somewhat to the problem but we need to look at the specific problem and identify the 'specific' cause of the problem before we lay the blame on any particular star.

In this particular case and based on my own research, the #5 Yellow in this case actually mitigated the problem and reduced the potential for what could have been an even more disastrous situation in the kitchen. A 'fire' caused by a weak 4 and 9 combination is easily overcomed by large quantities of Earth – which the #5 Yellow provided. Hence, the mishap was not serious and the damage was limited to one heavily charred chicken.

While it is important to examine the sources of Classical Feng Shui, it's important to remember that the information in these texts should not be considered literally or without consideration for the individual situations.

Understanding Your Destiny, Changing Your Life

I have met many enthusiasts who have learnt Feng Shui, researched it and studied it diligently, then applied it religiously taking into account all the monthly and annual changes in the Stars and Qi flow.

And yet....nothing happened.

They saw no effects. In drastic cases, things even got worse. And they were thus left wondering – why and where did they go wrong? Or is it simply that Feng Shui does not work?

Sometimes, we tend to forget the concept of balance. Feng Shui still works on the basic principles of Yin and Yang. After having studied Feng Shui, some enthusiasts will proceed to enhance the wealth stars within

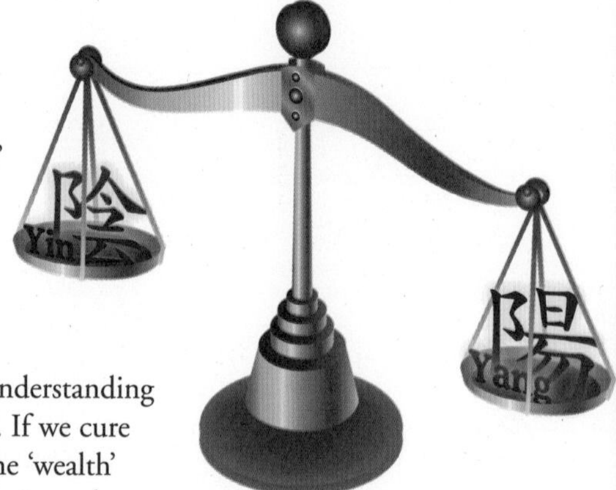

their home or office directly, hoping to increase their 'wealth' luck. While this is a step in the right direction, at times, unknowingly it is possible to go overboard with this as well.

Often, this is due to a lack of understanding about the real problem at hand. If we cure the problem at the root, then the 'wealth' aspect of our lives will fall nicely into place. Meaning, instead of 'enhancing wealth', we solve or cure an existing 'problem' that has been impacting on the wealth issue. The wealth then improves as an indirect result. It even seems to happen naturally.

When attempting to bolster a person's financial luck, his Destiny Chart or BaZi is sometimes overlooked. Destiny or Heaven Luck, influences 33 percent of a person's life. Feng Shui or Earth Luck, influences another 33 percent. Man Luck or a person's own actions makes up the final 33 percent. A person's Destiny or Heaven Luck is determined at birth and is evaluated by examining his BaZi or Eight Characters (Chinese Astrology Birth Chart).

A person may already have the 'wealth luck' in his chart but it may often be obstructed by other current issues in his life. If instead of addressing those issues, a practitioner just proceeds to enhance the wealth elements in the person's home or office through Feng Shui, you may very well see the person's health deteriorate as a result or other problems arising.

天
HEAVEN
地
EARTH
人
MAN

Why? The basic principle of balance has been overlooked. Balance is the key. Too much of a good thing can bring about negative effects.

For example, we know water 'enhances' wood. But add TOO MUCH water and wood will 'float' or rot.

By identifying the root cause of the problem, then applying the right Feng Shui cure to rectify, it will indirectly bring about an overall improvement in the 'wealth luck' of a person and other areas of his life. A good analogy is a doctor and

his patient. If the doctor merely prescribed aspirin because the patient complained of a headache, without determining the real problem, it could very well lead to serious complications later on for the poor patient.

Feng Shui is a tool that helps cure a problem or empower a person to achieve his full potential. But a Feng Shui practitioner still needs to know WHAT the problem is and where his client's real potential lies before proceeding to implement any short or long term cures. To know what the problem is and the person's potential, his BaZi chart must be examined.

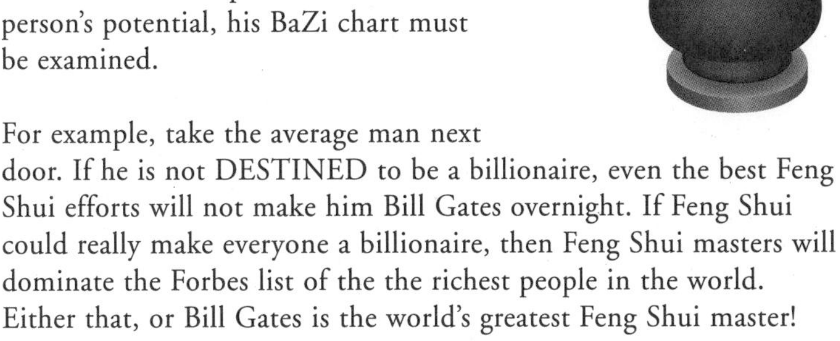

For example, take the average man next door. If he is not DESTINED to be a billionaire, even the best Feng Shui efforts will not make him Bill Gates overnight. If Feng Shui could really make everyone a billionaire, then Feng Shui masters will dominate the Forbes list of the the richest people in the world. Either that, or Bill Gates is the world's greatest Feng Shui master!

If a person is destined to only have a negligible chance of making very large sums of money or is unable to manage it, then strong wealth-centered formulas (Water Formulas for example) will only bring this person more trouble.

There is also a famous saying "too much wealth, deteriorates the health". 'Forcing' wealth Qi into the person's life is not the right cure if his Destiny does not or cannot support an increase in wealth. It might make matters worse.

A person's Destiny structure determines the capacity for wealth. If you want to change this capacity, you need to prescribe the right cure. 'Directly' enhancing wealth, most of the

time, is not the right way. First we need to extend and improve the main 'structure', then and only then can we increase the capacity.

The formula must match the person. In this way, a practitioner will also be able to advise his client on what actions he needs to take to achieve his goals and ambitions. All this analysis can only be done by using a person's BaZi chart and mapping out the person's destiny and life path.

The right prescription can only follow after a proper system of diagnosis. A BaZi chart is crucial to any Feng Shui consultation because it helps a Feng Shui practitioner understand a problem from the inside-out. Problems are then addressed with a clearer understanding of what is preventing a person from achieving his full potential, be it wealth or career or any other area.

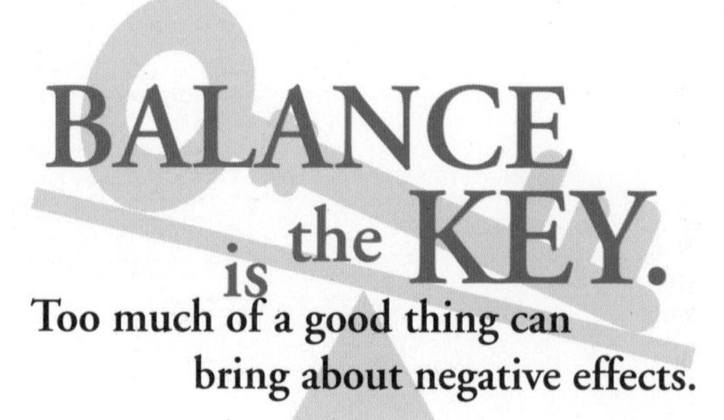

BaZi and Feng Shui - Distant Cousins?

Man is always fascinated by the great mysteries of life. Often, we wonder what our purpose in this world is. For centuries, the Chinese have studied this question of the 'Meaning of Life' and accumulated much knowledge in the course of their research.

By studying the interaction between Man, the environment, time and the Universe (often called Heaven), a pattern began to appear to the sages. This pattern represents the cyclical influence of the energies in the Universe imprinted on us during the time of our birth. This information is encrypted or coded in the form of Eight Characters (BaZi 八字). Thus the study and practice of BaZi calculation is to allow us to decrypt this code and reveal our destiny.

BaZi is like a diagnostic method designed to understand the condition of the patient or the person. Feng Shui is like a prescription used to treat a problem or condition the person may be suffering from. It is common knowledge that many well known Feng Shui Masters are also BaZi Masters. Or at least, they are good in one form of a Destiny analysis technique, like Purple Star (Zi Wei 紫微) System.

First Destiny, Second Luck, Third Feng Shui

The Eight Characters or Ba Zi represents the static chart of our destiny. (The eight characters are called our 'Ming' or Life.) Our Life Path or Destiny is calculated in what we call the dynamic pillars where they represent 10-year periods of our life. These pillars are known as Luck Pillars.

Luck Pillars can be considered the Luck factor. If we have a good natal chart (Good Life Chart), we need to be supported by the right luck in order for its true potential to be realised. Conversely, a mediocre Life Chart can be helped by a good set of Luck Pillars.

With a good Life Chart, Bad Luck Pillars are not too ruinous as opposed to a Bad Life Chart entering Bad Luck Pillars. The bumpy roads and smooth sailing journeys of our life, all depend on the quality of our Luck Pillars. Each Pillar is made up of two Characters: a Heavenly Stem and an Earthly Branch. Their elements generally govern the 10 years of a person's life with the influence being more pronounced in the Heaven Stem for the first 5 years and the Earthly Branch for the subsequent 5 years.

FENG SHUI?
BAZI?

A common question often asked by students is this: Do I need to study BaZi in order to practice Feng Shui? So, it was no surprise to me when a student posed this question to me over lunch the other day.

'The answer is simple really', I explained to the student. 'You can practice Feng Shui without studying BaZi but studying BaZi allows you to be truly effective in applying your knowledge of Feng Shui.'

It is said that Destiny comes first, then Luck, then only Feng Shui. Not knowing your capabilities or potentials makes it harder to know what lies ahead for you. BaZi is similar to a diagnosis provided by a doctor. Feng Shui can be likened to a prescription to manage your Destiny.

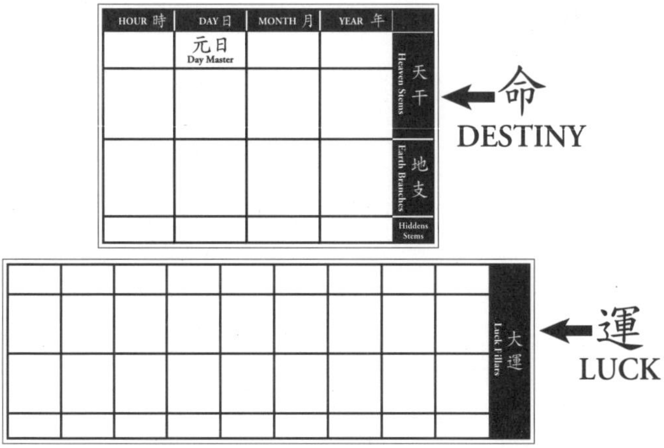

HOUR 時	DAY 日	MONTH 月	YEAR 年	
	元日 Day Master			Heaven Stems 天干
				Earth Branches 地支
				Hiddens Stems

← 命 DESTINY

									Luck Pillars 大運

← 運 LUCK

A BaZi (Four Pillars) chart

'How will you know what prescription to use without getting a diagnosis first?', I put forth the question to him. 'In case you did not know, most acknowledged teachers and masters of Feng Shui are masters in BaZi as well. Why do you think that is?'

Although it is not absolutely compulsory for you to study BaZi in order to practice Feng Shui, by gaining proficiency in BaZi, you can take your skills and application of Feng Shui even further. Of course a true expert in Feng Shui is able to read most symptoms from the Feng Shui of the property alone, however, they should understand that there are limitations because Feng Shui is not a system designed specifically to analyze Destiny. It is the same with BaZi, we cannot 'use' BaZi to do Feng Shui as it is a system designed to analyze Destiny, not Feng Shui. But these two systems complement each other.

Just as studying Mathematics makes it simpler when studying and applying the knowledge of Physics, so too does the study of BaZi remove certain obstacles in the practice and study of Highly Advanced Feng Shui.

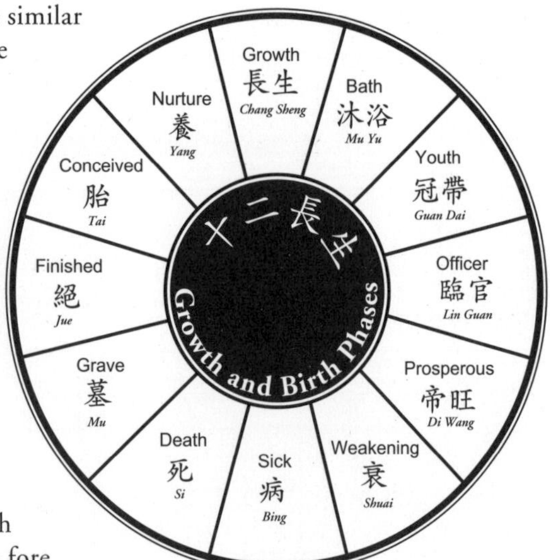

BaZi unlocks many doors in Feng Shui. For example, a lot of San He (Three Harmony) Formulas are similar to the formulas from the Four Pillars of Destiny. One of them is the 12 Growth Phases. This is what many people refer to as 'Secret' Water Dragon Methods - widely known as the water that creates wealth. But not many know that the basics and fundamentals are from the same BaZi Ming Li studies of the 12 Growth Phases of Qi. By having fore knowledge on these principles, the water formulas become much clearer and a student can immediately recognize and understand the true meaning behind the formulas. Some formulas seem 'illogical' or even wrong when you look at them only from the Feng Shui perspective because the original author of the ancient book may have written it in a way that presumed 'prior' knowledge on other subjects such as BaZi's 12 Growth Phases.

Furthermore, the Stems and Branches in BaZi bear a relationship to Feng Shui as they are very similar in Feng Shui studies. Even something as basic as the Five Element Cycle which is used extensively in Feng Shui applications is not fully unlocked until you study this in BaZi.

You may be familiar with the Five Elements but do you know which of these elements produces the fastest? How about which one produces the slowest? Does Earth produce Metal faster or does Metal produce Water faster? I asked the student further.

With an understanding of BaZi, you will not only know which element is the fastest producing element, but also understand when an element will produce, when it will not, how does an element get weakened, when it does not.

BaZi studies equip students with firm and thorough understanding of Five Elements. The relationship between each element is different. A clash between Yin Fire and Yang Metal is totally different from a clash between Yang Metal and Yang Wood. Although Feng Shui and BaZi are separate studies, knowledge of both compliments Feng Shui techniques and improves their application.

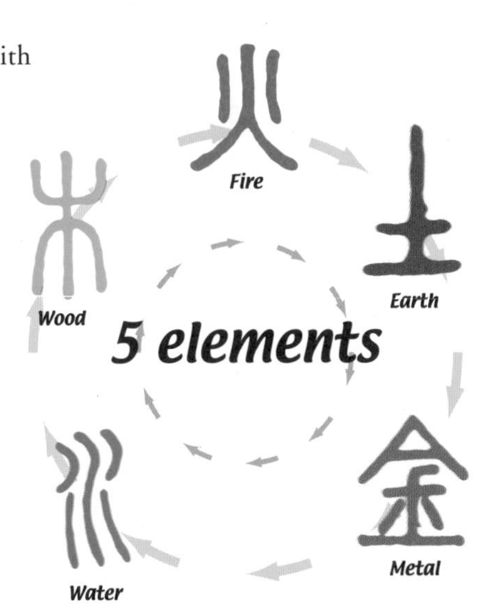

Why the need to study our destiny?

- It helps you plan your Feng Shui prescription for the long term.

- It helps in making informed decisions
  - by understanding our cycle of good and bad fortune, we are able to undertake proper planning and execute the right decisions that bring us the best possible outcome.

- Let's maximize our potential
  - We can capitalize on good luck cycles for entrepreneurial ventures or investment decisions.
  - We can reduce risk by being cautious and reducing our exposure during downward cycles.

- Understanding relationships, understanding others
  - People react and respond differently to different people in different time periods. By understanding the cosmic relation between yourself and your family or partner, you can foster better communication and improve relationships.

- Choosing the right career
  - Knowing which type of career or industry is suitable for you could be a very important step in your life. Why not choose a career where you can perform at your peak, where you'd enjoy your work and where you can excel?

- Interacting with people around you
  - BaZi allows us to understand the influence of people around you in your family or at work. Undoubtedly, we are very much influenced by our group of friends and family. Who is helpful and who is unknowingly impeding your progress?

Are You a Goat?

Once a month, I make it a point to catch up with some close friends whom I don't often get to meet due to my hectic traveling and teaching schedule. We usually have dim-sum or meet to 'yum-cha'(which is the Chinese version of sitting at a café and chatting away).

On this occasion, my friend brought along three of his lady friends. I had never met them before but when they heard that I was into Chinese Astrology, naturally, they were hoping I would be able to peer into their future for them.

Anyone who's an Astrologer or does Astrology for a living would have experienced this at some point or other. An acquaintance or friend expects some tips on his life over tea or dinner. And if you're not as willing to vouch information or give them a generous dose of 'you'll-be-the-next-Bill-Gates', they will write you off as a snob.

It's not that I don't want to give people advice or tips on how to improve their lives but it could very well end up to be the most expensive tip they ever receive. By this, I mean that looking at one small aspect of their lives without considering the 'big picture' and then acting upon it could very well lead to a lot of disappointment.

Anyway, Girl A looks at me and proudly proclaims that she's a Dragon. Girl B says, 'I'm born in the year of the Snake', and Girl C says she's a Horse.

In Spice Girls fashion, all of them asked me in unison, "Tell me about me!".

And then they all looked at me expectantly, almost willing me to give them each a reading that went along the lines of 'you will marry a good, rich husband and spend the rest of your life lounging at the country club and doing high tea with your girlfriends'.

How many people were **Born** in the **Same Year** as you?
ONE Million? TWO Million? TEN Million?

I explained to them that without a clear date and time of birth, any predictions I made might as well be a joke.

“Errrr - you’re not much of an Astrologer are you?”, Girl C enquired teasingly.

Girl A decided to read her own horoscope, “If the books can do it, why can’t you? I’m a Dragon you know. This year is bound to be good for me!”. She was beaming and it was with a heavy heart (well, almost heavy) that I decided to tell them the truth.

So, I asked them, “How many people were born in the same year as you? One million? Two million? Ten million?”.

“Is it possible all of them will behave the same way as you? Even your classmates, born in the same year as you could not have all been similar to each other”.

They nodded with puzzled looks on their faces.

How many people in the world are born in the year of the dog?

It's not uncommon for people to look up their animal signs and read all about the nice traits that they are supposedly endowed with, having been born under that particular animal sign.

Recently, one site I visited said that people born in the year of the Dog 'act from a deep sense of loyalty and honesty, and inspire confidence because they can keep secrets'.

Do people who are born in the year of the pig... oink?

Now, I am inclined to disagree with this general notion.

All people can have a sense of loyalty and honesty, not only those born in the year of the Dog. What if someone is now born in the year of the Pig? Do we expect them to be well-rounded, greedy and oink once in a while?

The problem today is that people see Chinese Astrology as just another section right next to the Sunday Comics. Walk into any bookstore these days and you'll see rows upon rows of books on Chinese Animal Astrology. Almost 95 percent of them concentrate solely on the personality traits of the twelve zodiac animal signs.

Chinese Animal personality traits describing the dog as loyal and the rat as a hoarder are not serious Chinese Astrology. These traits are written based on the perception of what the REAL animal may behave like 'if they were in human form'.

Have you seen a person oink or breathe fire? (Well, maybe some Dragon ladies but that's another story.)

Let me tell you where the 12 Animal Signs REALLY originates from.

You see, in the olden days, not many people had the benefit of a formal education. The animal signs we keep referring to, were thus used as a metaphor to help people remember the 12 Earthly Branches (Shi Er Di Zhi) used in Chinese Astrology and Feng Shui.

These 12 Characters, Zi 子, Chou 丑, Yin 寅, Mao 卯, Chen 辰, Si 巳, Wu 午, Wei 未, Shen 申, You 酉, Xu 戌 and Hai 亥, actually carry many intricate meanings about Qi, where the aspects of time and elements are concerned. In Chinese Metaphysical studies, they are consistently used as references in analysis and calculations. Since it was difficult for ordinary folk to remember them, the scholars of old assigned each character an animal symbology that gave it a visual representation.

So, when an ancient astrologer said "The Ox will encounter bad luck", they meant that those born with the Chou 丑 Earth Branch in their Birth Chart would encounter difficulties because the Qi of the year is not beneficial to them.

Over time, this Animal symbology took a life of its own. People began to attach animalistic traits to those born under a certain animal sign. Very soon, Astrology became inapplicable, as the true knowledge of it became muddled with the irrelevant information found in the Sunday newspapers.

ANIMAL SIGNS are ONLY used as a reference to the 12 Earthly Branches. 十二生肖

In fact, Chinese Astrology is a highly sophisticated study. There are two forms of Chinese Astrology that are widely used today, one is "BaZi 八字 " (Eight Characters or Four Pillars of Destiny) and the other "Zi Wei Dou Shu 紫微斗數 " (Purple Star Astrology). Both these systems take into account the year, month, day and time of birth so every individual will have a different chart.

The Animal Signs are ONLY used as a reference to the 12 Earthly Branches. It is possible to assess Qi influence and yearly influences based on a person's animal branch but it is not possible to do so with a great level of accuracy. Neither is it possible to ascertain characteristics or personality traits based on the Animal Sign alone.

So, the next time you pick up a magazine and it says people born under the year of the Goat or Ox are destined to eat grass and work hard, you know what to think!

Who is My Lucky Star?

"Are Dragons really luckier than other animal signs?", a concerned parent asked me the other day. She felt that her son, born in January in the year 2000, was 'unfortunate' as he missed being born in the Year of the Dragon. "He's a Rabbit", she said. She was worried and asked me what she could do.

As parents, it is a natural instinct to want to ensure that our children are either born with or given the best possible advantages in life. Hence, whenever a Year of the Dragon rolls around, there's no shortage of couples wanting to have a child. Chinese myths and legends may have something to do with this preference. Dragons have always been viewed as symbols of power and benevolence. In ancient China, the Dragon was a symbol of the Emperor and could only be worn on the attire of those in very high positions in the Imperial Court.

Although times may have changed, it seems culture has not and people still tend to think those born in the Year of the Dragon as 'luckier' than those born in other animal years.

To separate the truth from fiction on this matter, we need to turn to Chinese Astrology or BaZi. In BaZi, a person's Destiny chart is made up of 'Eight Characters'.

時 **HOUR**	日 **DAY**	月 **MONTH**	年 **YEAR**	
才 Indirect Wealth	元日	印 Direct Resourse	食 Eating God	**Heaven Stems** 天干
丙 *Bing* Yang Fire	壬 *Ren* Yang Water	辛 *Xin* Yin Metal	甲 *Jia* Yang Wood	
午 *Wu* **Hourse** Yang Fire	子 *Zi* **Rat** Yang Water	未 *Wei* **Goat** Yin Earth	申 *Shen* **Monkey** Yang Metal	**Earth Branches** 地支
丁己	癸	乙己丁	戊庚壬	**Hiddens Stems**

A BaZi chart

A Destiny chart consists of four columns which represent the Year, Month, Day and Hour of Birth. Each column is known as a 'Pillar'. Hence BaZi is often called Four Pillars of Destiny.

Each Pillar is made up of two characters, the top character is known as the 'Heavenly Stem' while the bottom character is referred to as the 'Earthly Branch.' A person's Animal Year is but ONE of the Eight Characters in a person's Destiny Chart.

Accordingly, from a mathematical perspective, the animal sign of an individual accounts for less than 12.5% of a person's Destiny chart and has more or less the same impact on a person's destiny. Yet, so much importance is placed on this one factor! By everyone!

The animal signs are really a layman's term for the Earthly Branches in a person's destiny chart. In the ancient days, when not everyone had the benefit of a formal education, symbolic references were the only way to explain complicated astrological terms to the simple masses, which consisted mainly of farmers and laborers.

The personality attributes tied in to the animal sign are a more recent invention, more for "entertainment purposes" rather than to provide any accurate astrological information.

Authentic Chinese Astrology is not read based on these 'animal signs.' People born in the year of the Dog are not more 'loyal' than those born in the year of the Goat or Snake. After all, people born in the year of Rabbit do not necessarily regard carrots as their favorite food! The animal signs are only references of the 12 Earthly Branches, nothing more.

"How about compatibility then?" the boy's parent asked. "A friend told me that my Rabbit son would get along well with a Pig and a Goat".

What she was referring to, probably inadvertently, is what is known in BaZi as the '3 Combinations' of Earthly Branches. The combinations have been simplified in the following chart:

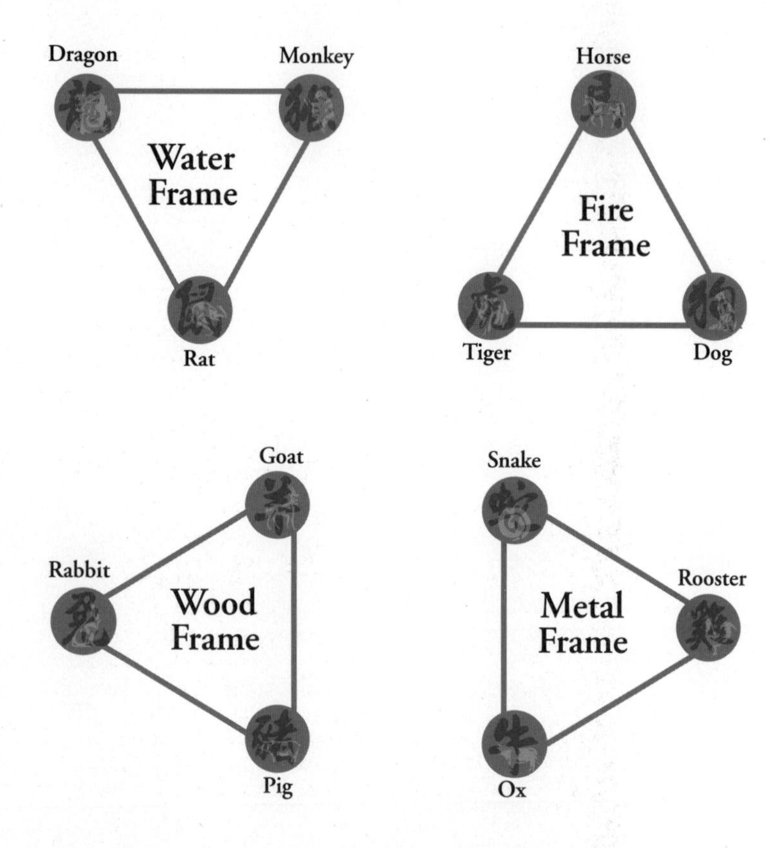

The three combinations are ELEMENTAL relationships between one branch and another. They are used in a BaZi (Four Pillars of Destiny) Analysis to determine how the branches react with each other (be it the Year, Month, Day, Hour) or whom a branch reacts to based on the Luck Cycle and Year cycles.

It is a common misunderstanding that these combinations refer to the so-called 'secret helpers' or 'secret helpful people' that each animal sign supposedly has. There is no such concept in BaZi.

When analyzing a person's BaZi chart, the 'helpful people' (the correct term in BaZi is Noble People) are not determined by the animal year alone. It is crucial that references are also made to the Day of Birth, in addition to the Year of Birth and Month of Birth.

As for compatibility analysis, the WHOLE Destiny chart of a person needs to be read and compared with particular emphasis being placed on the Day Stem. Any comparison made using solely animal signs will be guess work, at best.

Earthly Branch 6 Clashes Table

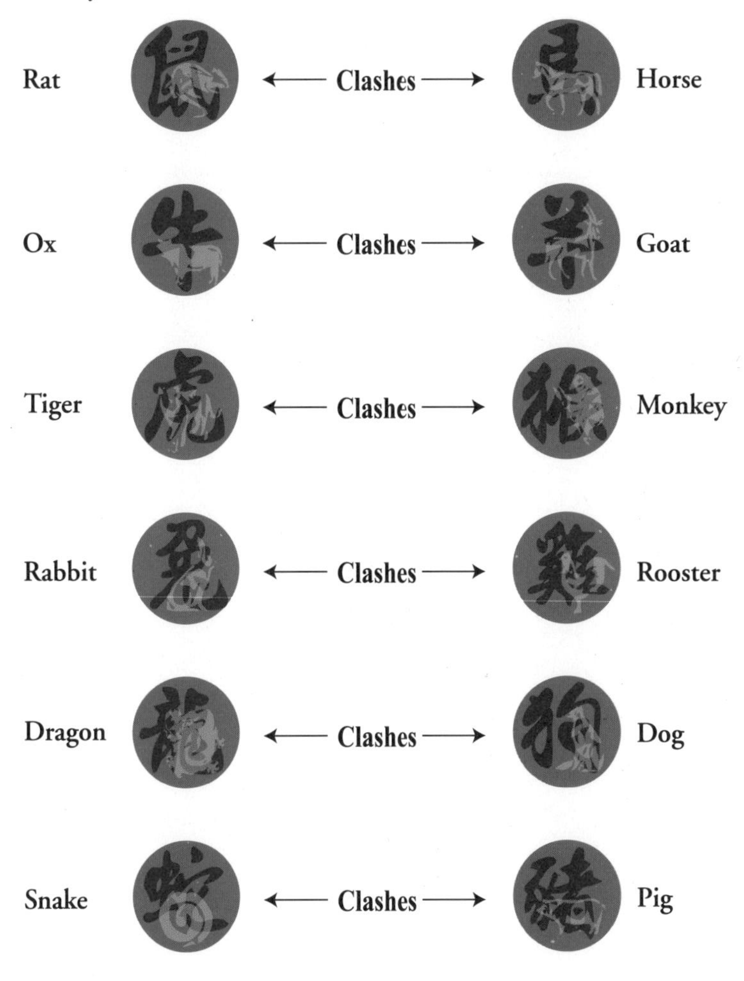

By the same token, there is nothing wrong with having friends who may be of the so-called 'opposite signs'. Some people misconstrue the fact that because certain Earthly Branches clash (the Rabbit and Rooster for example), thus having friends born in 'clashing' animal years will have a negative effect on them. In the study of BaZi, these people are not considered as being necessarily 'incompatible'.

So what of the mother who wanted a Dragon Son? As we can see from BaZi, a person's characteristics, attitudes and outlook in life are not based solely on the animal sign of his or her year of birth. I reassured the anxious mother that being born in the Year of the Rabbit was not necessarily a negative thing for her son. Being born in the Year of the Dragon is not in itself any guarantee of success in life!

Finding the Noble Man

Finding the Noble Man Star is one of the easiest applications in BaZi or Four Pillars of Destiny study and is a common question during any BaZi consultation. Nearly all the BaZi Consultations I have undertaken entail a question about Noble People in their lives.

The Noble Man Star, known in Chinese as 'Gui Ren Xing' is used to determine if a person will have 'helpful people' in their lives. Now, it is important to realise that this concept of 'helpful people' is NOT what is sometimes referred to as a 'Secret Helper' or 'Secret People'.

Noble Man Stars denote the presence of individuals who appear to lend you a hand, provide you with support or simply assist you in resolving a problem or difficulty at a timely moment. Often they may only make an appearance during a crisis or when you get yourself into hot soup.

In some cases, if the Noble Man star is strong and 'useful' in your chart, these special people can contribute towards ensuring nobility, fame and prosperity in your life.

How do you know if these people are or will be in your life?

First, identify your 'Day Master' by plotting your personal BaZi chart. (Use Joey Yap's BaZi Ming Pan Calculator at **www.masteryacademy.com**). Your Day Master is the Element in the top half of your chart, in the third Pillar from the right. (see illustration below)

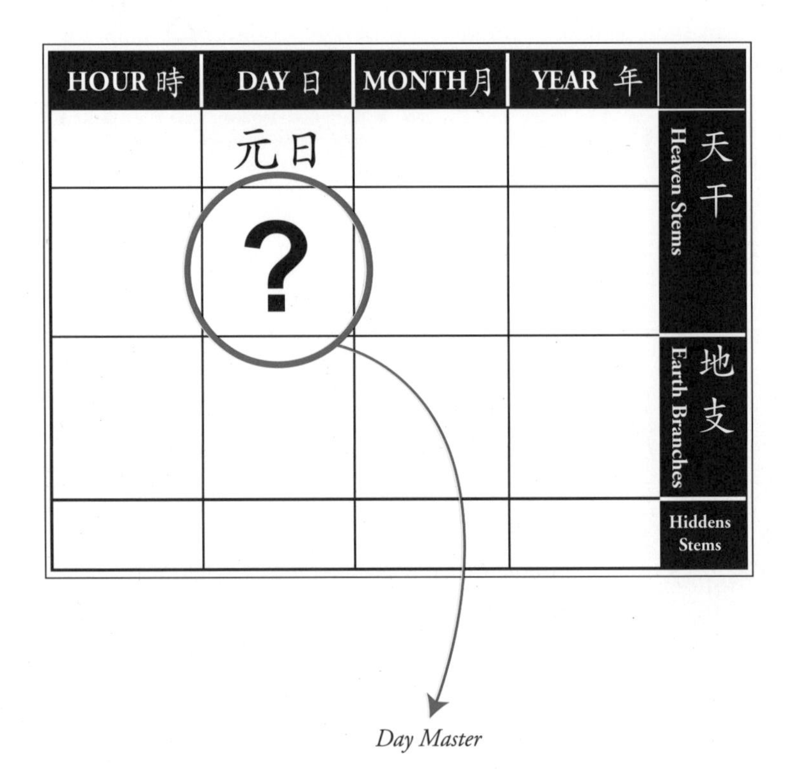

Day Master

Finding your Noble Man Star 天乙貴人

Day Master	Noble Man Star
甲 Yang Wood 戊 Yang Earth 庚 Yang Metal	Ox and Goat
乙 Yin Wood 己 Yin Earth	Rat and Monkey
丙 Yang Fire 丁 Yin Fire	Pig and Rooster
壬 Yang Water 癸 Yin Water	Rabbit and Snake
辛 Yin Metal	Horse and Tiger

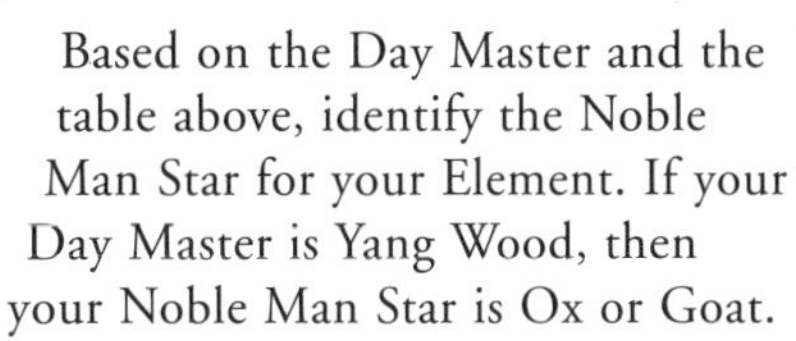

Based on the Day Master and the table above, identify the Noble Man Star for your Element. If your Day Master is Yang Wood, then your Noble Man Star is Ox or Goat. Now, how do you find this Ox or Goat? Look at the lower half of the BaZi chart (known as the Earthly Branches) to see if there is a Ox or Goat present.

If these stars are in your destiny chart, then you have 'noble' people in your life.

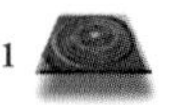

What if you can't find the Noble Man Star? Relax it's not the end of the world.

What if you can't find the Noble Man Star? Relax – it's not the end of the world. Yes, it may mean that during times of crisis or when you land in hot soup, you don't have someone extending that little helping hand. BUT, there may be other factors in an individual's BaZi chart that can help them, in their own way, deal with the situation.

Do keep in mind that this is a generic explanation of the Noble Man Star application. A professional BaZi practitioner and full consultation will yield more information or more details about the Noble Man Star.

#2 #3 = Bullfight Sha?

Recently, I did a Feng Shui consultation for a client who was also a student of Feng Shui and who had studied Flying Star Feng Shui.When I proceeded to make my recommendations at the end of the consultation, my client was surprised that my recommendations did not include asking him to sleep in a different bedroom.

You see, he had plotted his own house Flying Star chart and found that he and his wife were sleeping in the #2-#3 sector, a combination that is also known as 'Bullfight Sha'.

He asked me why I had not made any suggestions with regards to his bedroom or even recommended a cure for the 'Bullfight Sha'.

"There is no need to", I told him.

He was not too happy with this answer. He had read somewhere that his wife would divorce him due to the effect of the #2-#3 combination in his bedroom.

To set his mind at ease, I asked him if he had made a comfortable 7 figure income last year. He was taken aback and asked me how I had guessed so accurately (they lived a very modest life and were a happy, simple couple; no one would have even remotely guessed that they were millionaires). I pointed out to him that this very bedroom had brought him good luck for over 9 years since he and his wife had been living there.

He thought it over for a while and agreed wholeheartedly.

How did I arrive at the conclusion that my client and his wife would not be facing any serious relationship problems even though they were sleeping in the dreaded 'Bullfight Sha' room? Based on his BaZi chart.

My client's BaZi or Destiny chart clearly indicated he was a person who loved his wife deeply. It was not hard to see that they were a couple destined to grow old together – in Chinese, we say it is a Romance Made in Heaven. Hence my confidence in saying that the Flying Star combination in their bedroom will not break their marriage.

In fact, the combination more aptly fits "one above many" or high status in work and achievements, as seen from the hexagram as a whole, one Yang line amongst five Yin lines.

Upon further analysis of his BaZi, I ascertained that he might be headed for a possible major accident in the following year. My worries were confirmed when I cross-referenced this to the home's Xuan Kong chart. You see, a person's Destiny Chart will always correspond to the Xuan Kong of his house.

We then took steps to ensure that this possible mishap was brought under control. By applying Feng Shui there is a greater probability that this situation would not be as severe.

BaZi and Feng Shui are tools that go hand in hand. Attempting to provide a prescription without a clear picture of the diagnosis is only dangerous guesswork, at best.

BaZi is the methodology that we employ to diagnose the illness, Feng Shui is the medicine we then prescribe. The goal of the practitioner is to understand the problem from the inside-out and a Destiny chart helps the practitioner understand what they are working with, so that they can apply Feng Shui more appropriately.

Personally, I've studied and practiced BaZi, Zi Wei (Purple Star Astrology) and Mian Xiang (Face Reading). As a practitioner, I find that BaZi helps me greatly as a complementary system to my Xuan Kong. It assists me in understanding my clients, their needs and their problems better. This deeper insight allows me more options when I go about making my recommendations that work towards solving their problems.

Water Feng Shui

Many people know that Water is an important aspect of Feng Shui. It is said " Qi is dispersed by the Winds and gathers at the boundaries of Water." Clearly, Water is of paramount importance to the Feng Shui of a property but not many people know that Water is not just a case of having H_20 in your house or property (otherwise, a glass of water will make everyone rich!).

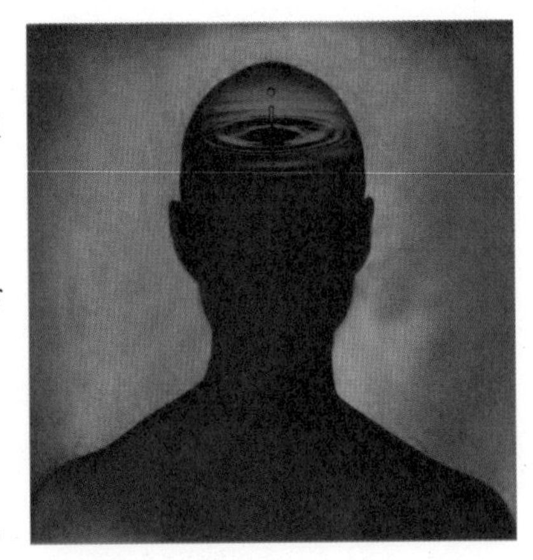

Not all Water is created equal. There are different 'types' of water with different qualities and characteristics. For every type of Water, there is a distinct character, which establishes its structure. Curved water, straight water, rippling water, rushing water are but different types of characteristics. Generally, there are five basic characteristics of Water corresponding to the Five Elements. Each is further divided into its Yin and Yang form.

When analyzing Water in Feng Shui, Feng Shui Practitioners will always consider the following points:

Is the Water Active or Quiet?

Moving water is naturally classified as Active Water. Examples of Active Water include rivers and seas. Man-made water such as swimming pools and aquariums are usually classified as Quiet Water.

Is the Structure of the Water Conforming or Non-Conforming?

This is usually an issue when examining Water in relation to a Mountain Embrace. If the left embrace is longer and water is flowing from left across the formation, then this is called non-conforming water. This formation is said to be of a lower quality. Where a Green Dragon is longer, ideally, water should flow from the right. This is called conforming water structure. Conversely, when the right embrace is longer than the left, and water flows from right across the formation, this is a non-conforming water structure. In such a case, ideally water should come from the left.

Is the Water Sentimental or Merciless?

Water streams that curve gently or meander are considered sentimental and such water will embrace lovingly the property and when it leaves, it gives the appearance of reluctance. This is a good form of Water. On the other hand, if Water rushes or gushes from a property or flows in a fast or direct stream towards the property, this is termed Merciless Water. Merciless Water is not only a poor conductor of Sheng Qi, but may actually harbour Sha Qi.

Is the Water Sheng Qi Water?

According to the principles of San Yuan Feng Shui, a landform must receive water from Early and Later Heaven positions. This denotes the receipt of benevolent Qi. In Xuan Kong Gua, water should be divided into Upper and Lower Yuan categories. Lower Yuan of 6,7,8 and 9 should receive water from 1,2,3 and 4 luck guas. This is called receiving Sheng Wang Qi (Growing and Prosperous Qi).

The most important skill for a practitioner is to be able to take his/her own experience and knowledge in the formulas and wield the factors like the Yin/Yang Five Elements, Ba Gua, Xuan Kong Gua in accordance with the Luan Tou (Environmental Factors) to determine the flow of Water.

Remember the key phrase ... there are no dead mountains, only dead water. There are no dead Water, only wrong Direction. If a practitioner can wield these three factors masterfully, any property can serve a Feng Shui purpose.

Blind Theory

Water formulas are a tricky business. They require very exact calculations and application of formulae and even then so many other requirements make it positively a Russian roulette game for the inexperienced. If the formula works, you get a good outcome. If the formula is wrong, we're talking bankruptcy. So it is not only a tricky, but very serious business.

I once met an acquaintance at a Chinese New Year party. He looked haggard and stressed. I gathered that things were not going well. I casually inquired how things were and out it all came, like gushing water from a leaking pipe.

He recently applied a water formula. "By the book", he said, "Just as the formula prescribed, exact degree, exact entry and exit. Just like I was told. I don't have a million dollars yet....I have more to lose - my mother-in-law's medical bills and car repair bills to pay". It almost seemed like he was reading me a very expensive menu after he had eaten the food.

My acquaintance was under the impression that Water formulas override all other Feng Shui formulas and theories (I assume he was referring to the traditional 8 Mansions and Flying Stars).

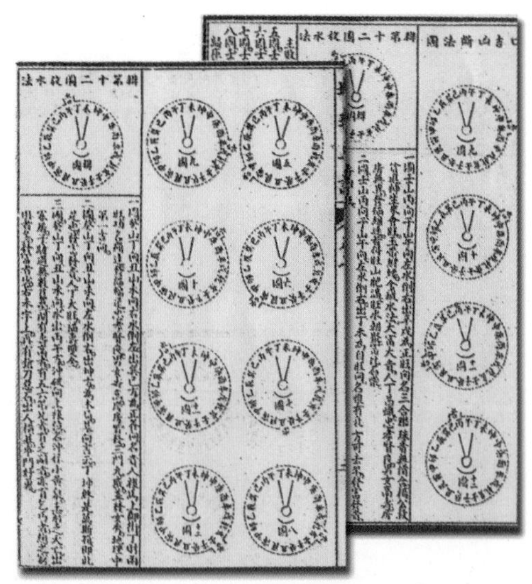

Copy of Water Dragon scripts from the Di Li Wu Jue 地理五訣 classics.

"This application was supposed to make me millions of dollars", he argued. "Instead, my mother-in-law broke her hips; I had a terrible car accident costing me a fortune and on top of all that my boss wants me to take a pay cut or leave!"

It was pretty obvious he wasn't going to let me leave the party till he got a straight answer from me!

- His house faces N2 (both Heaven and Earth plates)

- His water feature – from left to right, bypasses his front door. Exiting at a specifically given degree of 42 degrees, (Heaven Plate Chou (Ox) direction).

- Water enters from 240 degrees – SW3 (Heaven plate).

- Our water formulae enthusiast started constructing it in 2002 and it was completed in January 2003. By late January 2003, it was to be all systems go for the making of a wealthy millionaire (according to his idea of a Water dragon).

- He also sleeps in a Northwest room.

As I began probing his application a bit more, it became obvious what he had done wrong. I naturally asked him if he had considered the Flying Stars when building the Water structure. He shook his head and indicated that he was given the impression that it was not important where Water Feng Shui was concerned. First big mistake!

I also learned that he was born in 1961 – Gua #3 and born in the year of the Metal Ox (Xin Chou). He was also facing his 'Heavenly Doctor' direction, which he rightly believed to be good. But here's the real analysis:

- House Facing North 2 in Period 7:
  North East palace, has a 5-9 combination. Water is then exiting at the #9 facing star. This star, as we get closer to Period 8, is already a very important star. It governs 'potential' money related matters, business and investment relations. Water going OUT here, 'pushes' away this benevolent Qi and also, this ia a Direct Spirit 正神 location. Water should not exit here.

- Secondly, Ox, is HIS own life's animal sign. Meaning, it is HIS Tai-Sui. He has water exiting at his own Tai Sui. This year is the Year of the Goat. Goat clashes with his life as well as with his water exit.

This water setup was not suitable for him. He was heartbroken, to say the least.

What's the moral of the story then? Different structures have varying requirements when applying water formulas. Although the formula may appear to be the same, the application is usually quite different. A property must first be 'qualified' for Water to be used because not every property will benefit from such an application.

If the land is not 'fit' to have water, even with the correct formula in place, it will still be ineffective. His was such a case. The property is simply not conducive for a Water formation.

As pure Yang cannot exist, neither can pure Yin on its own. Think about it, can we ONLY have water without mountains? This factor needs to be satisfied in order to be a so-called 'millionaire-producing' structure. The quality of such a site also determines the eventual outcome of this formula. Such formations are, unfortunately, rare and few. Finding such a structure these days is a real problem.

In this present setup that he has, Water comes in from the South West 3 quadrant of the Heaven Plate. This is coming from the '3' Period Luck according to Da Gua and is not regarded as the right type of Qi to usher into your home based on his house's Xuan Kong Da Gua structure. To put it simply, it is out of favour.

Next, when you consider advance 'Life Palace' and 'Shifting Palace' Xuan Kong analysis, the #2 star has entered the #1 Kan at the door. The Kan palace houses the #3 Base Star, which in this case, represents him.

Upon 'shifting' the secondary star (Qi) into the Central and re-flying it in the grid, you will find that the #9 star (which was originally hurt by the water exit of the house) has entered the Xun palace. Among other things, the Xun palace represents the hips.

He Tu principles indicate that the #9 and #4 tend to combine – a successful combination will result in Metal. This Metal is said to 'hurt' Wood. The Gua that is affected is #2 because it has 'revealed' itself in the Kan palace. In this case the #2 represents his mother-in-law.

SE	S	SW
巽 xun	離 li	坤 kun
E 震 zhen		兑 dui W
艮 gen	坎 kan	乾 qian
NE	N	NW

The #8 star, which represents the limbs and back of the body, encounters the #9 star this month. The original 'metal' star #7 has entered the actual Kun palace (according to Shifting Palace method), meeting with the original annual and monthly 3-2. Not to forget, he is in the North West room with the original 3-2 meeting the monthly#7. The stars there indicate trouble as well. So I believe that his mother-in-law may have also hurt her hands and limbs in the fall.

His car accident is easily derived as well. His own Gua, Life Palace and Bedroom are all indicative of this. The excessively strong Wood Qi encounters a very strong clash in the form of Metal Qi. Such an interaction between these elements indicates possible road accidents.

By the end of my whole discourse, I could see that he was looking for a solution to his problem – not just a reason as to why things weren't working out.

In this case, with not many options left, the easiest way to alleviate some of the problems is to stop the Water. Then move the door to another sector so that things will improve even further when Period 8 rolls around. After some of the Feng Shui advice, I also recommended he not to take things at face value from now on. Water Feng Shui is complicated. Studying it is the easy part, application takes time to master.

Water. It's a tricky business.

Exploring the Castle Gate

I got a phone call shortly before the premier viewing of Lord of the Rings: The Return of the King, from an anxious and distraught student this year.

"What can I do for you?" I asked, pulling my socks on – my mind on the film. She explained to me that she was apparently in a muddle with her client and she needed information to complete her consultation.

"I need to use the 'Castle Gate' and I need to 'steal' the water."

Eh? I paused from thoughts of Elves and Middle Earth, straight into Feng Shui mode.

"What do you mean by 'stealing' water exactly?" I asked her, trying to figure out where she was coming from.

"Well, err.... according to what I had been taught, it is 'stealing' the water, am I right? I was also told that all that was needed was to 'fly the stars Yin' and we'll receive the water star at the water, right?" she asked, sounding terribly confused.

Unfortunately, it's common for students to pick up wrong theories – when this happens, it's important to nip it in the bud before it gets out of hand. I felt here was an opportunity for me to explain to her that this was not the right concept and to set her on the correct path.

I could almost hear her exhale in relief while I said, "Now let me explain..."

The ancient classic "Dou Tian Bao Zhao Jing 都天寶照經" puts it this way:

Five Star 1 Verse is not real,
Castle Gate 1 Verse is the truth,
Having the 5 Stars Castle Gate Verse,
House or Grave will be very auspicious.

As you can see, the verse says that 'Five Star Verse is not real' for the Early Heaven Ba Gua is about polarity and Qi. It does not deal in what is 'coming' or 'going' because it is the body and structure of

Qi. So for application, it needs to be jointly used with the Later Heaven Ba Gua.

- That's why from the Five Stars (which refers to the Five Elements mainly) transforms into the 9 Stars.

- From the Five Stars - we then go into or apply the Castle Gate theory.

- When establishing the Facing for the Castle Gate - remember this verse 'Water converges at the front, Facing use reverse, Water converges at the back, Facing take clockwise. Two corner Castle Gate receiving water, Borrow Yin calculation position to establish victory'

- The last two lines clearly discuss the 'Castle Gate' theory.

- Where water converges on the adjacent palaces of the facing direction, there is a possibility of assessing the quality of the water by flying the Base Star of the palace. If the corresponding water receives the 'prosperous star' of the period, this denotes a potential for great wealth.

"As you can see," I casually explained to the student, "Castle Gate theory is used to assess the quality of the body of water and not to be used as an application formula to 'steal' the water."

The base number that is flown might not always fly 'Yin' as it is popularly thought of. "You need to know when and how."

Of course, one also needs to observe the He Tu numbers (this is the verse's reference on the Five Stars). The He Tu numbers are 'related' palaces in the Lo Shu diagram. They represent the pre-ordeal Qi connection between one palace and the other. Their respective Qi penetrates one another, and if the Castle Gate appears in the 'related' palaces, the Qi is pure. If it doesn't, you can be sure the Qi isn't going to last.

You also do need to be positively sure of the existence of a Castle Gate formation before you apply a Castle Gate Theory.

The Castle Gate and the Castle Gate Theory are two entirely different things yet they also need to correspond with each other.

One last bit of information to keep in mind: The Castle Gate Theory emphasizes on positions of water, and there is an Internal and External Castle Gate formation based on the Castle Gate Theory.

After that phone call and juggling act to dress up, I made my way to the cinema with my close friends and spent a luxurious time watching Lord of The Rings. While watching a section in the film of a castle gate being breached, I smiled to myself and thought, "now isn't that a coincidence?"

Early and Later Heaven Water – Open Sesame!

'Water' is a very crucial component in the study and practice of Feng Shui. Water allows Qi to converge and collect. It can direct, move and activate Qi. But it is exactly this ability of Water to gather Qi that it is often mistaken as being representative of 'wealth'. This is not an accurate interpretation.

In the Five Element theory, Water represents 'Wisdom' and 'Intelligence'. When the potential for 'wisdom' is maximized or completely realized, then 'wealth' can be attained.

In the practice of Feng Shui, there are many 'Water Methods'. One of the more popular methods known as Early and Later Heaven Water.

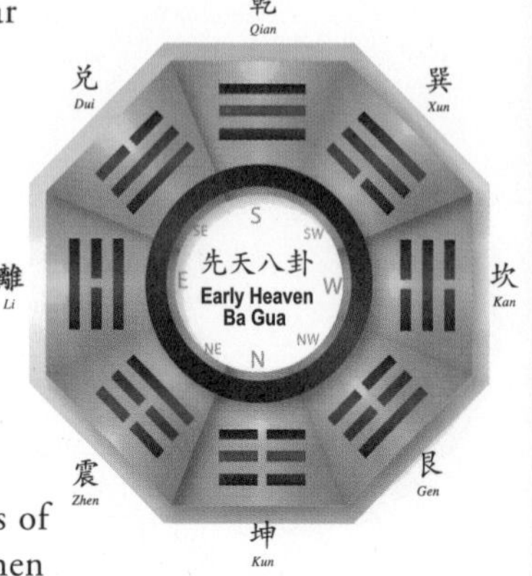

The Early and Later Heaven Water is a methodology that belongs to the San Yuan's Long Men Ba Da Ju (Dragon Gate Eight Formation) School. A pre-requisite to understanding this system of Water Feng Shui is a clear grasp of the 'One Palace Three Mountain Ba Gua' concept. These corresponding Three Rings of the San Yuan Luo Pan need to be noted when applying this theory.

The Later Heaven Ba Gua is also known as the 8 Palaces, where each palace governs Three Mountains. For example, the Kan Gua governs Ren, Zi, Gui – three mountains.

There are two ways in which this formula can be applied. The first is in accordance with the Big Ba Gua where the Directional Palaces are used as a reference. The alternate, more sophisticated technique is the 64 Hexagrams in the form of Xuan Kong Da Gua.

In the General Ba Gua Formula, each Gua governs Three Palaces. The Early and Later Heaven Position is as follows:

- Li Gua : Early Heaven is Zhen and Later Heaven is Qian
- Kan Gua: Early Heaven is Dui and Later Heaven is Kun
- Qian Gua: Early Heaven is Li and Later Heaven is Gen

The Early Heaven Gua governs its own mountains. For example, the Early Heaven Dui Gua, is from the Xun until the Mao Mountain.

The Early Heaven Qian Gua is from the Wu mountain until the Xun Mountain.

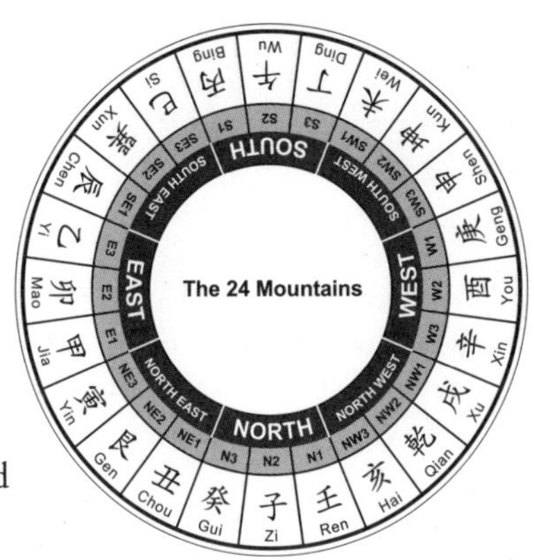

Each 'Palace' has got three mountains, and each Mountain governs 2 Hexagrams.

Generally speaking, the Early and Later Heaven Guas can be categorized into 8 sets.

- Qian Group – Early Heaven in Li, Later Heaven in Gen
- Dui Group – Early Heaven in Kan and Later Heaven in Xun
- Li Group – Early Heaven in Zhen and Later Heaven in Qian
- Xun Group – Early Heaven in Kun and Later Heaven in Dui
- Zhen Group – Early Heaven in Gen and Later Heaven in Li
- Gen Group – Early Heaven in Qian and Later Heaven in Zhen
- Kan Group – Early Heaven in Dui and Later Heaven in Kun
- Kun Group – Early Heaven in Kan and Later Heaven in Xun

The Guas within the same group can penetrate its own Qi. Meaning, there is an inter-connection of Qi within its own group.

So how can these Gua 'connect' the Qi? The method lies in the Xuan Kong Da Gua's 'Cheng Gua' or formed Hexagram. The main Eight Hexagrams are "Qian, Dui, Li, Zhen, Zun, Kan, Gen and Kun".

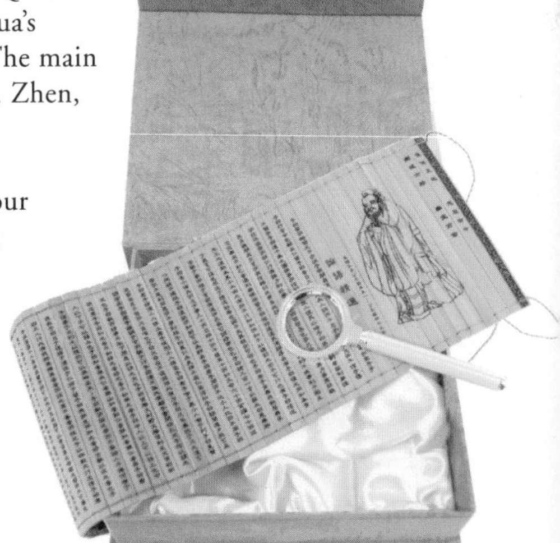

If the Early Heaven Water reaches your Bright Hall, this is regarded as being desirable. Of course, this assumes that it does not 'violate' the Early Heaven Water structure. Later Heaven governs wealth and career aspects. If this water is received, it helps in fostering prosperity luck for the residents.

Naturally, it would be ideal to receive BOTH Early and Later Heaven Water.

The force of influence of the Early Heaven and Later Heaven Water received depends to a great extent on the quality of the Xuan Kong Da Gua formation that supplies it. If the Gua Yun is coupled with the correct Gua formation, then the Qi is said to flow unobstructed and smoothly, fostering prosperity for many generations.

It is also important to observe the mountain formations. These must conform to the Da Gua principles in order to realize 100% of the Early Heaven and Later Heaven water's effects. The support of the land itself is crucial. Simply adhering to the formula itself is only about 60% of the formation's power. The 'key' triggering factor lies in the clever arrangement which taps into the external mountain formations.

Finally, one must not forget the basic San Yuan principle of Ling Zheng (Direct and Indirect Spirit). This principle is the core, the backbone of San Yuan water methods.

In the practice of **FENG SHUI,**
there are many **'WATER METHODS'**

Mistakes are often made when practitioners overlook the following:

- Ling Zheng principle.

- Fan Fu Yin – as the Heavenly or Earthly Guas are the same, especially in the form of Water, Dragon, Sitting or Facing. If these enter Fan Fu Yin formation, usually the effect of the Early Heaven and Later Heaven cannot be realized or its effectiveness is, at least, reduced by half.

- Out of Gua formation – when the receiving of water does not belong to the same group, it means that there is no connection of Qi and therefore the benefits or setbacks will not be felt by the residents.

Zhen Yin, Zhen Yang (Real Yin, Real Yang)

真陰

真陽

The main concept of Real Yin, Real Yang, Zhen Yin Zheng Yang stemmed from an old Taoist Art called NEI DAN. According to its explanation, it emphasized that "a real YANG originated from the YIN; a real YIN is formed from the YANG". (Note: not to be confused with Pure Yin 淨陰 and Pure Yang 淨陽).

The Nei Dan text explanation on the concept of Yin and Yang converges on the understanding of Qi in our internal body. In the study of Feng Shui, Yin and Yang is reflected in our natural world as the River, Mountain, Earth and Man.

So how does this concept of Yin and Yang affect Feng Shui methods, you ask?

Real YIN VS Real YANG

the concept is actually based on dualism. No one force can exist without the other.

According to Master Jiang's explanation in his Di Li Bian Zheng book, in Feng Shui, Sheng Qi (growing Qi) comes from YIN but is dominated by YANG.

What does this mean exactly? In Feng Shui, the concept of Yin and Yang symbolizes the forces of Tian Di (heaven and earth). Sheng Qi that meanders on Earth is said to come from Heaven.

There are 9 Stars (different variations of Yin and Yang) that control, govern and activate this Sheng Qi. The flow of this Qi influences the order of the universe and lives of the human beings on Earth. A practitioner must understand how this Real Yin and Real Yang works in order for him or her to successfully manipulate, enhance or redirect Qi.

The relations and interrelations between the forces of Yin and Yang, coupled with the principles of the Five Elements and the Ba Gua gave rise to the many theories of Feng Shui. According to Jiang Da Hong, this formed the basis of Xuan Kong Da Wu Xing (Great Xuan Kong Five Elements) and Xuan Kong Da Gua (Xuan Kong Great Hexagrams).

Within the Yin there is Yang and within the Yang there is Yin. What is this concept and how is it useful in our Feng Shui practice?

What it means is actually macro vs. microseism and the duality of every form of energy. A Yang form of energy like a #8 Facing Star (although mainly Yang) can be in Yang form or in Yin Form. If #8 is active, it is in its Yang form. If it is supported by the right forms - it is in its Yang Form. If it is inactive or unsupported by the right forms - it is in its Yin form. In that 'state', the #8 star can again be classified into its Yin or Yang form and so forth.

The theory of Real Yin and Real Yang also extends to the concept of 'going with the flow'. Meaning, where extreme Yin is found, one should not be 'balancing' it with Yang, but rather, the right thing to do, is to let it be more Yin. Similarly, in an extreme state of Yang, one should let it be Yang. For example, where presence of Yang Metal Qi is overwhelmingly strong, one should not bring balance by using Water (to reduce its strength) but rather, let it be even stronger by using more metal.

Real Yin vs. Real Yang - the concept is actually based on dualism. No one force can exist without the other. Without Yin there is no Yang and without Yang there is no Yin. Translated into Feng Shui practice, a property cannot have good Feng Shui without internal and external collaboration of Qi. Internal layout of Qi must match the External layout structure. This is the concept of Yin and Yang. In microseism, External factors like Rivers must match with Mountain (Yin/Yang) and Internal Factors (open space vs closed space, door location vs desk/sleeping location) all play an important aspect. Every star in the 9 Stars has a dominant Yin/Yang nature. But as an individual star, it will have yet its own Yin and Yang traits. In order to understand Xuan Kong Feng Shui, one must understand the Yin and Yang nature of the Stars. In different timings, each star exerts different levels of Qi. But in different Yin and Yang conditions, their abilities can be heightened, weakened or altered.

Every star can be noble and hostile. According to the concept of Real Yin and Real Yang, every star is related to one another. Its Yin and Yang nature would affect a neighboring star and produce certain outcomes.

The next time you do your study in Feng Shui, try and analyse the formulas in terms of its Yin and Yang perspective. Studying a formula from its roots helps you with your understanding when it comes to application. Every formula has a 'purpose'. Once you understand how a formula was formulated, you will understand its purpose and its application better.

Walking the Mountains in the Home of Feng Shui

In 2004, I took a large group of students to China to learn Feng Shui by "Walking the Mountains". A large number of these students were westerners - the first westerners in the world probably to embark on an Imperial Feng Shui Tour, studying Yin Houses of the Emperors of the Qing Dynasty; "Walking the Mountains" and seeing how ancient Feng Shui masters tapped into the Dragon's Vein to find Qi powerspots. I had a great time showing my students not just these incredible Feng Shui sites, but the culture and the beautiful architecture of China.

Outside the Yong Ling Mausoleum, observing the Prostrating 'Table Mountain' Dragons in the vicinity with students of the Mastery Academy

Taking Luo Pan readings inside Yong Ling Mausoleum

Outside the Tomb of Emperor Qian Long with students of the Mastery Academy

The author at the entrance to Huang Tai Ji's Burial Ground

The author and his students at Bei Hai Park, in Shen Yang, the burial ground of Huang Tai Ji

The author at Bei Hai Park, in Shen Yang, the burial ground of Huang Tai Ji

The author and his students at the Forbidden City, Beijing

The author and his students at the Eastern Qing Tombs

Mastery Academy Students and Joey Yap at the Shen Yang Gu Gong

The author and his students discussing the Feng Shui of the Forbidden City at Jing Shan Hill.

Walking down from tombs at Fu Ling, Shen Yang

At the Fu Ling Tomb

Moderating a discussion on the White Tiger and Green Dragon land form embrace at the Yong Ling Tomb

Students evaluating the Feng Shui of the Shen Yang Gu Gong

At the Shen Yang Gu Gong, studying the Bright Hall

Observing the 3 Divide 3 Harmony formation at Zhao Ling Tomb

With students at Zhao Ling

Discussion outside Emperor ShunZi's tomb

With students at the Bright Hall of the Eastern Qing Tombs

Moderating the Feng Shui discussion at Zhao Ling

Showing students the Clipper Cutting Formation at the Shen Yang Gu Gong

At Yong He Lamasery, Beijing

A Feng Shui History Lesson

Once upon a time, there was a small tribe in the far east side of China called the Ju Zhen. Once they ruled the Yellow River but that did not last and they were soon reduced to a fragmented scattered group of rivaling tribes.

In 3 generations, this small band of tribes ascended to the throne as the Sons of Heaven and established the Qing Dynasty in the Forbidden City. With just about 500 men, the JuZhen, who had since changed their name to the Manchu, overthrew the ageing Ming Dynasty and established their own Dynasty that would rule for 260 years (1644-1911).

Nuerhachi

Now, historians of course will have their geo-political and socio-economic explanations for why the Manchus were able to overthrow the Ming Dynasty but I'm quite sure that there is no history book that talks about how Feng Shui helped to propel the Manchus from being a minority tribe into the rulers of China.

Yes, you read it right. Feng Shui played a part in helping the Manchus become Emperors and it all comes down to where the grandfather of this guy called Nuerhachi was buried.

When the Mountain makes an Emperor

Yong Ling's Dragon Veins

Yong Ling Mausoleum is not usually the sort of place tourists visit (unless they have some serious fascination with history or a few hours to kill). Located in Liao Ning Province (formerly known as Manchuria), you need to take a one-hour bus ride to get to the Mausoleum. But anybody who wants to study forms or Luan Tou and who wants to see what kind of environmental formations are needed to become an Emperor must visit Yong Ling.

When we talk about Yin House Feng Shui, we are talking about the Feng Shui around a person's grave. What is the difference in the Feng Shui of a Yin house and Yang House? The principles are the same, as my students discovered on their trip to China. It's just that in the case of Yin House Feng Shui, the inhabitants don't move out after they've moved in! The environmental features of the landforms analyzed and studied in 'Yin' Feng Shui are the sames ones used by 'Yang' Feng Shui. To truly understand classical Feng Shui, studying from the roots, which is Yin Feng Shui, is essential.

Now, if you want to be an Emperor, you need a bit more than a hill with a nice view for a grave.

You need a REAL mountain. But not just any mountain. A mountain with proper 'backbone' (or superior incoming dragon ranges) and with the RIGHT kind of Sha (砂) or Land form Embrace. You need to see nearby mountains around the designated site or spot that represents Officer Stars, an Imperial Seal, Flags and Drums that symbolize your army. You need Chastity Mountain veins as source dragons to create powerful, potentially ruthless individuals, not a typical Huge Door or Greedy Wolf Star Mountains which produce nice but goody goody two shoes types. And you need a nice strong Table Mountain, prostrating in the distance to lock in the powerful Qi from the Mountains and keep it circulating. And you need proper water formulaes to facilitate the flow of Qi.

Now you're wondering – Huge Door, Greedy Wolf, Flags and Drums – where do you find mountains that look like that? It's all a matter of training your eyes to see the shapes. In Feng Shui there is a saying: " A first-class master sees the Mountain (Stars), a second-rate master sees the Water, and a novice runs around the mountain and sees nothing."

That's why it is said that to become a true student of Feng Shui, you must 'Walk the Mountains'.

The Will of the Heaven – An Imperial Destiny

Prostrating table mountains at the front of the Yong Ling mausoleum

According to legend, the chieftain Nuerba (grandfather to Nuerhachi, who started the Qing Dynasty) was buried here in what is known as a "Burial By Heaven". After his death, his son, carrying an earthen urn containing the bones of Nuerba, stopped to rest at the present Yong Ling site while searching for a burial spot for Nuerba. He placed the urn between the roots of an Elm tree, then rode off to find a Feng Shui master to help him evaluate the site for burial.

The ancestral tablet halls at Yong Ling

By the time he came back with the Feng Shui master, the roots of the Elm had wrapped themselves around the urn, making removal impossible. The Feng Shui master then saw that the surrounding landscape, mountains and embrace formed what is known as a Reverse Dragon Facing its Ancestors (Hui Long Gu Zhu 回龍顧祖). Wisely, he told Nuerba's son to leave the urn there.

And the rest is history.

Nuerba's grandson, Nuerhachi, united the JuZhens, renamed them the Manchus, formed the Qing Dynasty and started the journey towards the Forbidden City in Beijing.

Now, there's always going to be some skeptics who call this a case of Feng Shui Reverse Engineering. Here's an interesting fact: the Qing Dynasty had 12 Emperors. The mountain where the Yong Ling Tomb is located has 12 humps.

The mountain where the Yong Ling Tomb is located has 12 humps

Coincidence? X-File? You might be thinking – is this true? Scientists don't just arrive at their conclusions based on one piece of evidence. Judges do not make their decisions based on one piece of evidence. We need to see the same outcome, the same conclusion, several times before we can say it is definitive. This goes along with Feng Shui and it has always been my teaching philosophy.

The burial spot in Yong Ling. Here lies the great ancestor of the Qing Emperors

Panoramic view from the Meridion spot of Yong Ling, looking outwards

As you read on, you will see that the history of the Qing Dynasty – its rise, its downfall, is all foretold and supported by the Feng Shui of their Yin and Yang Houses. Now when so many factors point to one conclusion, can we logically ignore it?

Fu Ling, Shen Yang

China: the Best Feng Shui in the world?

"China is the birth place of Feng Shui – so how can there be bad Feng Shui in China?" asked my student recently while we were climbing the Jing Shan hill behind the famed Forbidden City in Beijing during our recent Mastery Academy Imperial China Excursion.

Pavillion at the top of Jing Shan

The Forbidden City, Beijing

This question came after we had just spent 5 days 'walking the mountains' and doing hands-on live audits of many famous buildings (both Yin and Yang) from the Qing Dynasty Era, China's last Imperial Dynasty that spanned 263 years.

It is of course difficult for many people, even my own students who are dedicated students of Feng Shui, to accept that not only is there 'bad' Feng Shui in China, but it is bad in some buildings that were inhabited by Emperors.

The lakes and distant mountains (dragon veins) around the Forbidden City, Beijing

Hence, it's extremely important for students to not always just assume certain things when it comes to Feng Shui. On the Mastery Academy Imperial China Excursion, the whole point of the trip was for students to be able to see for themselves (by taking their own Luo Pan measurements and looking at the mountains and water landforms surrounding various palaces and tombs) that even Emperors, with the best Feng Shui brains advising them, could sometimes have bad Feng Shui. In the study of Feng Shui, nothing is constant. Some things that are good today may not be in the next hundred years. Likewise, bad Feng Shui can change over time.

The view of the Forbidden City from Jing Shen

The author with his students at Emporer Qian Long's Tomb

What kind of examples that we saw were bad Imperial Feng Shui?

Students were in for a surprise at Emperor Qian Long's tomb at the Eastern Qing Tombs in HeBei Province, 3 hours from Beijing. Emperor Qian Long, renowned in history as one of the greatest Qing Emperors, second only to his grandfather, Emperor Kang Xi, ruled for 60 years. His tomb is an extravagant, marbled structure built at great cost and is a shining example of bad Feng Shui despite the world's best advisors.

Aerial view of the Eastern Qing Tombs

Though the location of the tomb is aptly located at one of the three main veins of the main incoming dragons and was correctly tapping into the proper recoiling embracing arms of the left and right distant hills and protected by the rising mountain at the front, the tomb was mistakenly aligned in a detrimental axis.

You see, Emperor Qian Long's tomb faces what is known as a Death and Emptiness Line. On the Luo Pan, there are 24 directions, known as the 24 Mountains. If a property's Facing direction falls on a Death and Emptiness Line, that means it has no clear direction and therefore, it is not receiving any Qi. There are various types of Death and Emptiness lines, some are more serious that the others, while some are negligible.

We call this in Chinese – "Auspicious Land, Inauspicious Burial. (吉地凶葬 Ji Di Xiong Zang)"

A student measuring the direction of Emperor Qian Long's tomb

A student who was first sent to do the measurement was shocked that she measured this particular facing line for the tomb. She thought she made a mistake with the measurement. However, shortly after that, the whole group of us made the measurements and confirmed that it was slap on the direct Line of Death and Emptiness (空亡線 Kong Wang Lines).

Consequently, after Qian Long, all the subsequent Emperors of the Qing Dynasty performed poorly. Because the "area" (land) was still good, the good fortune stretched. But because the 'alignment' was wrong, it could not benefit, thereby no longer improving since Qian Long.

The last Bright Hall "明堂 "collects Qi for the Hall of Supreme Harmony at the Forbidden City

Then there is the Forbidden City. It has long been the seat of power for China's Emperors since the Ming Dynasty, but its Feng Shui is, as my students discovered, not as good as they expected it to be.

Feng Shui in the Forbidden City wasn't of course always bad Feng Shui – obviously, the Ming and Qing Empires lasted a good 200 years each – that's not too bad for an Empire. This is because Forbidden City receives the dragon vein from noted Chastity Star mountains rising from Hai 亥 (North West Palace). Hai 亥 is also the Tian Huang 天皇 (Heavenly Emperor) Star based on the 24

The Sheng Lung Dragon veins releases powerful meridian spots in which the Eastern Qing Tombs were positioned

Heavenly Star method of Feng Shui. This dragon, when verified along with the water position using Long Men Ba Da Ju formula, qualifies as a good incoming dragon. The six 'lakes' which form Bei Hai and Chong Nan Hai form an embracing water dragon around the palace – a Jade Belt of Qi. The Qi from the North Western mountains is gathered by the water formation created by the imperial forces and harnessed by the Forbidden City.

However, good incoming dragon needs to be accompanied with proper 'tapping' of Qi mouth and water in the Direct and Indirect Spirit locations is not beneficial during every Period. Time is one extremely important factor when it comes to Feng Shui. The main challenge for most Feng Shui masters is, how to establish a Feng Shui formation that can last as long as possible.

The key to the Feng Shui of the Forbidden City lies in the 'location' of the city itself. It is tapping into the Qi from the Northwestern incoming dragon. Water bodies are correctedly located externally and internally. The sophisticated interior lay - out of the Forbidden City serves to facilitate the flow of Qi from these external features.

Emperor Qian Long's tomb

View (looking outwards) from Emporer Qian Long's Tomb

The design of the San Fen San He (3 Layers of Separation and Combination) of Luan Tou formations are repeated in the design of the Forbidden City to circulate and coagulate Qi over the palace grounds.

Dragon motifs all over the Forbidden City. Feng Shui or Culture?

Yet the South East and North West water mouths and paths of the Forbidden City eventually led to the demise by 'hanging' of the last Ming Emperor. Why? In the study of Xuan Kong Flying Stars, "4-6" (South East and NorthWest) denotes death by hanging. This of course needs to be coupled by correct timing in the shift of the qualities of Qi during those years.

Table Mountain and Rising Mountain at the East Qing Tomb

The Forbidden City was significantly renovated and built up by the Qing Emperors after they moved their seat of power from Shen Yang to Beijing. Much of the decline of the Qing Dynasty was caused by over-meddling by female Dowagers and this is exacerbated by the higher White Tiger (Right side) and lower Green Dragon (Left Side) in the structure of the Forbidden City.

For the novice Feng Shui student, the Forbidden City poses an interesting question in this day of pop Feng Shui, when every problem and hassle can be 'cured' by some trinket or another. If you're someone who believe that objects like golden dragons or 5-clawed dragons, bronze tortoises and the like are all it takes to ensure prosperity, longevity and power, then you should ask yourself why despite living in a palace full of Dragons, 5-clawed and otherwise, tortoises and storks, that the Chinese Emperors in the end, met with such ignominy during their downfall?

Having seen this with their own eyes, my students now understand that even Chinese Emperors can be careless when it comes to Feng Shui. Feng Shui is an ongoing practice and a continuous learning process. Good Feng Shui can help the making of an empire and bad Feng Shui can hasten its downfall. Think about how important it is to be aware of the Feng Shui of your own home.

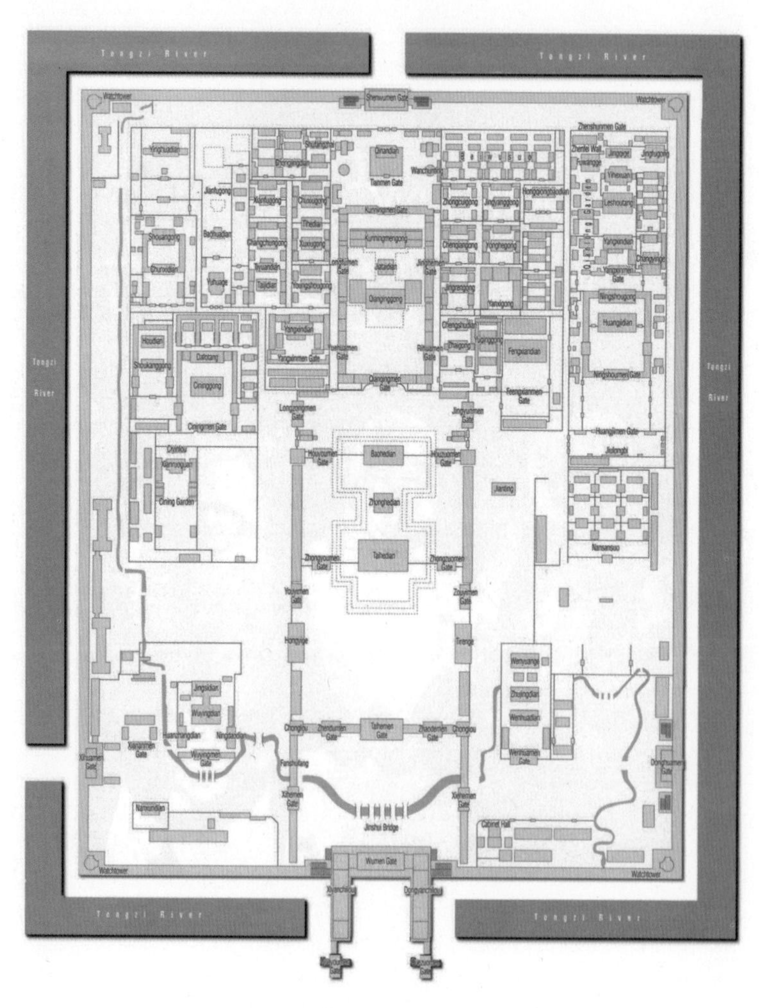

Map of Forbidden City

The Essense of White Tiger and Green Dragon Formations

A lot of Feng Shui books talk about the terms White Tiger and the Green Dragon. Most of them have tips on how you can 'make' your own White Tiger and Green Dragon (and Black Tortoise and Red Phoenix) and how these 'animals' can bring good fortune to a property. But many people don't really KNOW what a White Tiger and what a Green Dragon really is. Many regard these as the left and right of their gardens or better yet, think these refer to statues and figurines they need to place in the four corners of their homes.

These terms actually refer to the left and the right. Right is the White Tiger. Left is the Green Dragon.

Now, if you're asking yourself, right and left of what – you're on the right track. It is about the left 'embrace' or Sha 砂 and right embrace of the landforms in the vicinity of your property.

Now you might be asking yourself – embrace?

The author with his students at the Summer Palace

One of the inspirations behind the conception of the Mastery Academy Imperial China Excursion was to be able to show students, by making them "walk the mountains" (although these days, we take a bus), how the mountains have different shapes (like pen holder, sky horse, camel humps, imperial seals, officer stars) and also how the mountains form an embrace to hold in the Qi around a specific dragon vein (spot where Qi collects).

This picture shows the dominating high 'White Tiger' embrace at the Summer Palace, Beijing

The Summer Palace

By looking at the embrace of a mountain and the landform, a well-trained Feng Shui practitioner can tell a lot – at the basic level, a good embrace indicates that Qi is being well-collected and circulated. But an embrace will also tell whether or not, for example, women or men will be empowered and which son will likely inherit power.

The function of the landform embrace (sha shou), or what the layman terms it as the 'Green Dragon and White Tiger', is to protect the site from drastic sha Qi (strong winds that disperses the Qi), help coagulate Qi in the area and redirect water flow. The landform embrace around the property dictates the quality of the area.

Marble boat at the Summer Palace

During the excursion, students had the opportunity to look at several different embraces and to attempt to determine whether or not the White Tiger or Green Dragon was higher.

It is said in the ancient classics 寧可青龍高萬丈，不可白虎抬頭望 "It is better to have the Dragon higher by heaps than to have the Tiger peeping its head".

The Qing Dynasty was dominated by two women: the Empress of Huang Tai Ji, Empress Xiao Juang and the Empress Ci Xi. Huang Tai Ji's Empress is a lesser known Dowager, largely because she exercised her influence discreetly and highly benevolently. She had helped her husband Huang Tai Ji, her son, Emperor Shun Zi and her grandson Emperor Kang Xi.

Main entrance of the Summer Palace faces East

The Empress Ci Xi, who came to personify the word 'Dowager', is the one that most people know of or have heard of, thanks to her renowned extravagances – the Summer Palace, the Marble Boat.

What is the reason for this? One of the major factors lies in the quality of the landform embrace configurations of the mountains! In many locations visited by the students during the Imperial China Excursion, the White Tiger embrace was significantly higher than the Green Dragon, signifying 'woman power'. The Forbidden City in Beijing has a higher, more prominent White Tiger than Green Dragon. At Hetuala City, the former capital of the Manchus before Shen Yang, also has a slightly higher White Tiger.

Now it is not just the height of the White Tiger formation, it is also the 'quality' of the formation that spells out the actual power of this unique Feng Shui formation. The White Tiger embrace is usually marked by unique 'seals' flaunting the sides of the White Tiger or you could see 'sword' formations that signify 'authority supreme'. In some cases you can also see what we call 'phoenix tail' formations flagging the sides of these White Tiger formations. This is why we classify that the quality of the White Tiger embraces is significantly stronger than the dragons.

Hetuala City - former capital of the Qings

The steep back mountain behind the main palaces at the Summer Palace

And if you want to see an example of what I call White Tiger Overkill, then visit Empress Ci Xi's Summer Palace in Beijing, which has virtually no Green Dragon (explaining perhaps the lack of power of the 3 Emperors who lived during her reign as Dowager) and in fact, has a special Curling White Tiger embrace, which especially empowers women.

Now, you might be wondering: so now I know what a White Tiger and Green Dragon is – can I build one? Turn the page and you'll find out...

A Lesson on How to Make a Mountain!

Whenever I teach Flying Stars and talk about how 'forms influence the stars, and stars in turn influence the residents', people nod and think that their rock garden or maybe rocks in their koi pond are the mountains influencing their Mountain Stars. (Mountain Stars or Sitting Stars govern Relationships and People Luck).

Emperor Huang Tai Ji's Tomb

Main Qi Mouth of Zhao Ling

Sometimes, I do come across clients (and students) who proudly point to a little ten foot cement mountain, complete with gushing water fountain, outside their home and say 'look at my mountain'. Better yet, pictures and paintings of mountains it seems can make up for the lack of the real thing.

Now, my students who went on the Mastery Academy Imperial China Excursion have SEEN with their own eyes what it takes to make a mountain. To see it, you need to visit Shen Yang, the old Manchu capital located in Liao Ning Province and to go to what is known today as Bei Ling Park.

BeiLing Park is where the Zhao Ling Tomb or North Tomb is located. It is the location of the tomb of Huang TaiJi, the son of Nuerhachi and grandson of Nuerba. Although HuangTaiJi did not personally lead the conquest of the Mings, he did lay the foundations for the Qing Dynasty and thus, is regarded as a Qing Emperor.

Bei Ling Park, Shen Yang

Zhao Ling provides the answer to the oft-asked question: is it possible to MAKE a mountain and river, to create the landform that is needed to produce premium Feng Shui?

The answer is YES, but only if one can replicate it on the scale and extent in which it is found at Zhao Ling.

BeiLing Park is an extensive and large park area. To get to the tomb, you take a 4km ride on a buggy, and then cross through 3 large gates before arriving at the massive mould that is the tomb of Huang Tai Ji.

This artificial mountain took about 12 years to construct. Ground was removed to form two great bodies of water, which today, are lakes in BeiLing park. These acted as a barrier to collect Qi from the river in a distance since "Qi is dispersed by the wind, and gathers at the boundaries of water". At the same time, the bodies of water represent the application of the small taiji of the area's Luan Tou. The water feature was a lake that surrounds and embraces the front of the tomb.

The mound in Zhao Ling was made from the ground that was dug out. and is a Metal shape (Wu Qu 武曲) , thus signifying prowess in the area of Military Arts

Huang Tai Ji's Tomb: Zhao Ling

This potent example of what making a mountain means provided students with an inkling of just what a monumental task, making a mountain entails. Indeed, the notion that a rock or even a large boulder could represent a mountain was well and truly dispelled without doubt at Zhao Ling, as my students realised just what it means to 'make a mountain'.

Now, you can't just pile up a mould of sand as high as 10 stories and say, hah – now I have premium Feng Shui.

At Zhao Ling Tomb, the burial complex contains 3 Bright Halls (Ming Tang), which create the 3 Divide 3 Harmony 三分三合 (San Fen San He) aspect of the landform. The 3 layers of Bright Halls act to collect Qi, circulate it and send it into the tomb. The entire structure of the complex mimics the Sha or embrace of mountains. Surrounding the grave mound was a tilted walkway, which acted to ensure that the grave mound did not become waterlogged and which also functioned as the Cicada Wings 蟬翼 .

On the Cicada Wings

Most importantly, the mountain only works because it is a Flat Land Dragon 平洋龍 (Ping Yang Long) . What is this Flat Land Dragon? The principle of the Flat Land Dragon is that in a place that is completely flat, the structure that rises above the others will stand out and thus receive and draw all the Qi to it. According to flatland dragon theory, water pathways must be observed first to determine the 'low' dragon veins.

If you build your mountain properly, if you build it in a place where the Flat Land Dragon principle applies, then you can have superior Feng Shui. Just ask Emperor Huang Tai Ji, whose descendant luck was enjoyed by his grandson, Emperor Kang Xi (1662-1722). Emperor Kang Xi together with Emperor Qian Long (1736-1795), was regarded as one of the most skilled Qing Emperors and also one with the longest reign. Emperor Kang Xi reigned for 61 years, a reign matched only by Emperor Qian Long.

There are many more interesting aspects to the Feng Shui of Bei Ling. However most of it entails detailed explanations on sophisticated formulas and is beyond the scope of a simple Feng Shui book. If you are interested in some of these, please visit www.masteryacademy.com and click on the China Excursion articles to have a look.

From Joey Yap's Mailbag

Each week, I receive many questions from around the world about various facets of Feng Shui. I thought it would be fun to compile some of the more popular questions and also a selection of more technical questions, for those who have a deeper knowledge. It seems there are some serious misconceptions about Feng Shui out there! Have a read – perhaps your burning question has already been answered!

* *If you want to post your question for the next Stories and Lessons on Feng Shui book, send them to* ***questions@joeyyap.com***

Period 8 Anxiety

The end of 2003 and the onset of 2004 brought a flurry of emails into my mailbag – there was a lot of anxiety about Period 8!

I heard that people with Gua 8 will experience great snd tremendous success in Period 8. Is this true?

This theory holds no water and is too illogical. Think about it for a minute - IF this were true, then all Gua #7s in Period 7 would have been very lucky. Now, there were millions of people born under the year of Gua #7. Did all of them enjoy tremendous success in Period 7? Furthermore, if this theory was true, then would Gua #7 people need to wait 160 years for the 'next period 7' to enjoy any luck once again?

There is no such thing as a "more lucky than others" Gua number in any period!

Love: What's Feng Shui Got to Do With It?

Understandably, I get many, many, many questions on the subject of finding one's true love. It's sometimes difficult to answer because I don't want to shatter people's hopes but on the other hand, I do have a duty and responsibility not only to be honest but to give people the truth about what Feng Shui is all about...

I tried out a Feng Shui Love Ritual as outlined in a book for 49 days but nothing happened. Do I have to do the whole ritual again?

Feng Shui is not a spiritual practice and it does not require any 'rituals'. Feng Shui is science and a practice that enables you to tap into the Qi (natural energies) in your living environment. You need not perform any rituals or prepare magic potions to do so. In Classical Feng Shui, there is no such thing as a Love Ritual or any rituals for that matter.

If you want to increase your romance luck using Feng Shui, the simplest way is to try tapping into your personal Yan Nian sector. Alternatively, plot the Flying Star chart for your home and activate the #4 star for Relationship possibilities. Good luck!

I threw many Mandarin oranges into the lake this Chap Goh Mei. I am still waiting for my prospective husband to come into my life. Does it matter how many Mandarins I must throw for it to work? Or do I have to face a certain direction when throwing the oranges? What school of Feng Shui does this belong to?

Chap Goh Mei , which traditionally falls on the 15th Day of Chinese Lunar New Year, is also known as the Chinese Valentine's Day. A well-known cultural tradition of Chap Goh Mei is the throwing of mandarin oranges into the lake or river.

There's no harm in joining the fun and tradition. If you believe hard enough, it might just work. But this cultural practice does not belong to any Feng Shui school nor is it Feng Shui! It has no Feng Shui connotation whatsoever.

I have a bathroom in the South West sector of my house. I read a book that says that the South West is the relationship corner of the house. Am I flushing all my romantic luck down the toilet?

Good news! You'd be pleased to know that in Classical Feng Shui there is no such theory that states that "South West" is the universal definitive relationship corner. None of the hundreds of Feng Shui classics since the Tang Dynasty makes any historical reference to the South West sector being the "relationship" sector. This is probably misinformation caused by the surge of English books on Feng Shui in the last few years.

So no, you don't have to re-locate your toilet, stop using it or stop flushing it!

I was told that the South West sector is my love corner. What does this mean? How do I energize the South West sector?

The South West sector as the Universal Love Corner is a common fallacy stemming from incomplete Feng Shui information. The South West is not a "universal love" corner - there is absolutely no historical and theoretical basis to support it. You need not worry about what is in the South West and you can be rest assured that there is no need to energise it either.

Can you please tell me is it a Feng Shui fact or a superstitious belief for me to put a set of love candles in the South West corner? I am hoping that Feng Shui can bring me the love of my life but it's been 4 months now and nothing yet. Where's my man?

Unfortunately, the candles in the South West will not help you with finding Prince Charming or Mr Perfect. But if you really want to help Cupid, you will first need to identify your personal Yan Nian direction/sector and then proceed to try to tap into this sector/direction in your home.

Log on to www.masteryacademy.com for the Ba Zhai or 8 Mansions Calculator to find your Yan Nian Direction.

WANTED: Interior Decorator. Feng Shui Knowledge Preferred.

A close friend of mine who is an interior decorator recently showed up at one of my courses. He's found it tremendously useful for debunking strange request from clients. I get a lot of questions about placement of objects and beautiful ornaments in my mailbag – maybe I should take some lessons in interior decoration...

I recently bought a beautiful wooden hand-crafted dragon statue. I was told that dragons represent power and fame. Can you tell me where to put it for best results?

You can place the dragon anywhere that you feel is appropriate. Frankly, the placement of objects is not part of classical Feng Shui. It is the job of an interior decorator.

The dragon's effect on you is purely "psychological". If you believe it benefits you, it probably will. If you do not, then it's just something nice to display in the house. Bottom line: your dragon doesn't really have a "Feng Shui" effect.

A friend of mine bought me a beautiful antique vase. The little booklet that came with it says it was made during the Qing Dynasty during Emperor Qian Long's reign. Is it good luck or bad luck to own such an old item? And where should I place this vase?

It seems that you are concerned that the vase might carry with it some bad Qi left over from ancient times. If it does worry you and cause you unnecessary mental anguish, then I suggest taking the item to a temple (or any other spiritual place) for a cleansing. However if you don't feel anything negative about it, it is perfectly okay. Enjoy your antique!

Many wealthy people with a penchant for interior decoration of a historical bent enjoy buying and keeping antiques. I have a client who buys Emperor's robes and frames them up in his house as decoration. He keeps robes of Emperors that did well during their reign and even those that didn't.

At the end of the day, it's just a vase. It has no good or bad luck attached to it. As for placement, place it in a place that brings you joy to look at it because there's no Feng Shui significance to where you put it. If you're not sure, ask an interior decorator!

Dead Fish Tell No Tales

Ah, the fish. The truth is that Fish and Feng Shui only have one thing in common – they both begin with the letter 'F'. Still, it's one of the more well-entrenched Feng Shui myths around, which explains the proliferation of mail I get about pet fish, dead fish and the Number #1 question: what fish to get?

I had a beautiful Arowana in my home. I had it for 6 years and it was costly to maintain and keep the fish. My mother-in-law insists that this is a good luck fish. I personally cannot say it has brought me any special good luck nor bad luck. Recently the fish died and my family was quite disturbed. My mother-in-law was highly distressed, taking it to mean a bad omen from her deceased husband. Since we threw the deceased fish away in the rubbish bin, she thinks we've really botched up our Feng Shui. Can you please confirm if we are just being paranoid?

I'm sorry to hear about your Arowana pet. Please assure your mother-in-law that it is perfectly all right to get a new fish if the fish gives you pleasure to look at or you have an admiration for the beauty and elegance of the Arowana. There is certainly nothing wrong with rearing a beautiful Arowana. But please don't get another Arowana if you are not a pet fish lover and your only intentions are to treat it as a money-magnet.

Jokes aside, it's probably due to 'superstition' that your mother-in-law is concerned.

PS: There is nothing 'Feng Shui' (good or bad!) about the way you dispose of the carcass of the fish. So don't worry. It will not come back to haunt you.

Wealth, Women and Feng Shui

I think the phrase 'wine, women and song' should be replaced with Wealth, Women and Feng Shui. People always seem to associate Feng Shui with Wealth (getting more of it) and Women (husbands having too many!).

Ever since I read from a book that water on the right side of the door makes my husband have a roving eye, I am constantly worried. I do not understand why this is so yet I feel very uneasy. I keep suspecting infidelity by my husband and our relationship has been rather tense. I cannot remove the water because it is a pond in my neighbor's house compound. Please help.

The situation seems to be causing you a lot of needless heartache and no doubt, unnecessary stress for your husband.

It is not a Feng Shui theory that water on the 'right side' of the door causes infidelity. This 'theory' is not found in any of the respectable ancient Feng Shui classics. It's probably an old wives tale or just superstition.

You need to understand that 'water' is a source for Qi to gather and collect. Water on whichever side of the main door does not mean anything unless it activates or de-activates a type of Qi.

This myth has caused a lot of problems for couples because something that is not there ends up being created by the jealousy and suspicions of wives paranoid about water on the right. Relax, stop worrying, and concentrate on loving and trusting your husband. That in itself will most definitely improve things!

I tied the mystic love knot on the rose quartz stone in the South West corner as described exactly in a book. My hubby is still having an affair! It didn't help at all. What can I do? Please help.

No number of mystic knots is going to stop his philandering. Its help is mostly psychological. Instead, I suggest you focus your energies on checking two important things. First your Main Door and then your sleeping direction/location.

If your door is located in an unfavorable direction then you might want to consider using another entrance to the home that is favorable to you. This is by far a much more effective remedy than the rose quartz stone. Also, try to determine your Yan Nian direction and tap into this while you sleep or work.

To find your Yan Nian direction, use the Ba Zhai or 8 Mansions Calculator found at www.masteryacademy.com

Office Qi

Questions about career, promotion and of course, office seating are popular when it comes to Feng Shui in the office.Here are a few of the frequently asked questions (FAQ) from my mailbag.

I have a question about my office Feng Shui. My back is exposed to my office room door because I work facing the window. Do I need to place a mirror on the back of my chair to deflect the negative Qi?

The mirror is not going to be of much help to you. The solution is simple, really - all you need to do is keep your door closed while working.

The more important question here is are you facing your favorable direction while working? The door behind your back is not as dangerous as you tapping into the wrong direction while working.

Use the Eight Mansions calculator at www.masteryacademy.com to determine your auspicious directions. Depending on what boost you need (be it career, or perhaps more support from co-workers), tap into the appropriate direction.

I am concerned about having disturbed the Grand Duke Jupiter (Tai Sui) in my office. I was recently promoted and given a new office. I should be happy but then I just found out that my seat faces South West which is the direction of the Grand Duke. This book that I am reading says that it is bad luck to face the Grand Duke. I just got promoted and I don't want to sound superstitious to my boss. What can I place in my room to negate the effects of the Grand Duke?

Each year, certain directions are considered inauspicious because they can exert evil influences and are generally referred to as Sha Qi. Referred to as the San Sha, Tai Sui, and Sui Po, these portents of Sha Qi change directions and locations annually, the change coinciding with Li Chun, the annual beginning date of the Chinese Solar Calendar.

The Tai Sui, generally referred to as the Grand Duke of Jupiter, Grand General, or the Commander of the Year, is an intangible star which always corresponds directly to and occupies the Year Branch in any given year. The detrimental influence of the Tai Sui spans the entire 15° of the Year Branch.

Offending or disturbing the Tai Sui may cause various levels of effects including illness and injury. Minor effects could entail loss of money. Medical effects include blood-related injuries and loss of wealth. Extreme effects could entail severe injuries, calamities, and fatalities.

No doubt, Facing the Grand Duke puts you in a slightly disadvantageous position. However, if this direction of your office is not being renovated, then you need not worry. If the Tai Sui is not disturbed, it is usually not a problem.There is no need to 'negate' the Grand Duke.

Year	Grand Duke
2003	未 *Wei* **South West 1**
2004	申 *Shen* **South West 3**
2005	酉 *You* **West 2**
2006	戌 *Xu* **North West 1**

Year	Grand Duke
2007	亥 *Hai* **North West 3**
2008	子 *Zi* **North 2**
2009	丑 *Chou* **North East 1**
2010	寅 *Yin* **North East 3**

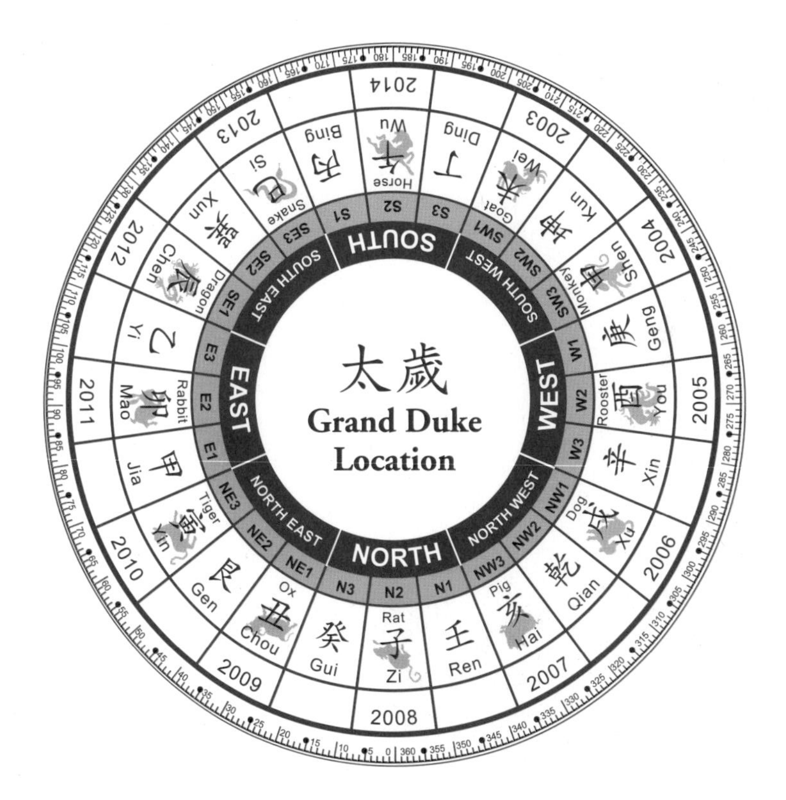

The key thing to remember when it comes to the Grand Duke is don't 'disturb' it by digging the ground that it occupie as this is Fan Sha (touching or against Sha).

And by the way, the Grand Duke does not occupy the whole of the Southwest area. Just the 'Goat' direction (you can find this out using a Luo Pan). So, if you are fortunate, you may not be facing this direction at all!

My family intends to renovate the house attic into a small office for my husband. The attic is located on the South West and the door at the top of the staircase leading to this attic faces north. My hubby's Gua is 4. Below the attic is the main toilet, a small living room with a fridge and kitchen cupboards. Would it be appropriate for him to run his business in this attic?

It's okay to run a business from the attic, although a larger room in the house would be more comfortable. Don't forget, Michael Dell of Dell Computers started from a dormitory and Jeff Bezos started his Amazon.com from a house garage.

As long as the Qi is good, flowing and unobstructed then there's no problem. You need not worry about the toilet and kitchen cupboard below the attic. Your main concern should be the energies in the South West this year.

Searching For Wang Qi

A week doesn't go by when I don't get something in the mailbox asking about money, wealth, how to create more wealth and of course, where the heck is this wealth corner!

There's so much contradicting information about Feng Shui out there - it's confused me! I heard that the wealth sector changes every year. Is this true?

This depends on which system of Feng Shui is used. I believe you are referring to the Flying Stars system. In this system you can ascertain the house's own wealth star location, which is fixed and does not move.

However, every year, there is also a visiting Wealth Star. The visiting Wealth Star, of course, moves from one location to another annually.

Annual Wealth Star Location

Year	Location
2004	North East
2005	South
2006	North
2007	South West
2008	East
2009	South East

I need to know if I can place a rotating crystal fountain to activate the wealth luck of my house?

旺氣

The crystal fountain is classified as 'moving water', meaning a 'Yang' feature. It is good for activating Qi. Based on the Flying Star chart of your home, locate the good facing stars for Period 8 (look for the Facing Stars #8, #9 or #1). You can then place your fountain in those sectors to help stimulate the Qi in those good areas.

Please note that a small table fountain contains only a little water. If your home is big or you seek greater results, you might want to consider a bigger water feature.

A Whole Lot of Wind

Wind chimes are easy to place in your house, look nice and perhaps have a larger-than-life nature when it comes to Feng Shui. Like fish, they seem to bring a lot of 'baggage' with them.

Is it necessary to refresh the 6-rod wind chime every year as advocated by some Feng Shui practitioners? This does not seem to make sense.

You are right. There is no logic in this. Unless of course, your Feng Shui practitioner wants to sell you another set of wind chimes every year.

The reason wind chimes are used is because we want to introduce Metal Qi into certain sectors. The question of 'refreshing' the Metal Cures does not even arise. Unless of course you are in a circumstance where the Metal Cure has rusted. You can continue to make use of your existing metal wind chime unless of course, you feel inclined to spend more money!

Do remember that there are many ways to introduce Metal Qi, and it may not need to be in the form of a wind chime. You may just as well use metal sculptures, trophies, pewter or copper plates.

My front door faces North and I've just realized the negative #5 Yellow star is lurking in my South East! Should I hang a 5 metal rod wind chime to neutralize it? Would a 6 metal rod or 7 metal rod wind chime be more effective?

A little knowledge is sometimes dangerous.

Unfortunately with Feng Shui, it has the tendency to frighten or disturb people needlessly, causing them to think the sky is about to fall on them unless they take some kind of action. I think it's much more important to understand the situation first before you do anything.

The idea of the wind chime in the South East was, I believe, to 'cure' the negative #5 Yellow star there this year (2003). But before you decide to do this, you must first determine if this is an important area in your home. If the South East sector of your home is only a storeroom, then you have no problem. Just leave it! Alternatively, you can decide just not to use that room or area for the year.

Feng Shui doesn't require you to go around enhancing and curing every corner of your house, CONTRARY to what many people think.

PS: If you DO decide to hang a wind chime, it needs to be made of metal. Having 5 or 6 rods doesn't matter as we are ONLY interested in the SOUND of Metal it produces.

I have a question about wind chimes. Do I have to use a 5-rod or a 6-rod wind chime to neutralise the #5 Yellow Sha?

It doesn't matter how many rods a wind chime contains, it does matter however that it produces a good "metallic" sound. What we want is the element "Metal".

In the study of the Chinese Five Element Theory, METAL is produced by EARTH. The #5 Yellow Sha is of the EARTH element. Having a wind chime in its sector redirects the negative energies of the Earth Five Yellow Sha to "produce" Metal. By producing Metal, it is weakened and therefore cannot cause much harm. That is why it doesn't matter how many rods a wind chime has, what does matter is that it be placed in the right location and that it makes a good metallic sound.

Do remember that when you are installing the wind chime, you DO NOT "nail" the ceiling or wall in case you activate your Three Killings or the #5 Yellow Star. It is best to "stick" your wind chime up without the nailing process. "Nailing" is a form of activation. The #5 Yellow Star must not be activated.

Colour Blind

When I do consultations, clients always ask what colour the walls should be painted in various parts of the house. They are invariably surprised when I say "Any colour you like". Don't be confused between superstition (black is funeral, white is the colour of mourning, red is prosperity) with Feng Shui. And also, do think about the big picture - the 'right' Feng Shui colour carries at best a 10 percent improvement to the Feng Shui of the room. Better a colour that makes you feel comfortable and relaxed than one you dislike and hate just for the sake of a miserable 10 extra percent.

My kitchen is in the South part of my house. The cabinets are in dark blue and beige. Is this an acceptable colour for them? I worry because the kitchen is a place for cooking and is of the Fire element. But my cabinets are in dark blue-water and beige – that represents Water right? I was told that the fire and water clash in this type of situation is not good. Does putting green plants all over the kitchen help?

Let me point you to the answer by asking you another question - which kitchen DOES NOT have Fire and Water? It is a fallacy that Fire and Water will automatically clash with each other. This is merely a description between two types of Qi.

In your case, you merely have cabinets in a particular colour – it will hardly be of any effect in real Feng Shui analysis. What matters most in your kitchen is where you locate your stove and where the 'fire mouth' is facing. The colour of the kitchen cabinets is yours to choose!

My kitchen located in the South West has sage green cabinets, stainless steel hardware and appliance fronts that also have black trim, top, or sides, stainless steel sink and fixture, counter top in greens and earth tones and terra cotta tile back splash. I have added four small accents in red that can be removed if necessary. But something is not right in that area, especially since the 2003 energies have come into play, but I can't place my finger on what is wrong.

Contrary to popular belief, colours do not have a very strong effect in Feng Shui. They carry, at most, a 5-10% influence. Colours may however have a strong mental and psychological affect on people.

Personally, I usually advise clients to use whatever colours they feel comfortable with and not be paranoid about using certain colours, as long as it makes them feel confortable. If your favorite colour is black and blue, go ahead and use them without constantly worrying about violating Feng Shui principles. If in doubt, just use neutral colours.

A feeling of uneasiness in the kitchen is most probably caused by the visiting #3 star (which may cause arguments and dispute). Your initial instinctive action to add RED into this sector is wise as red can represent the element of Fire. Fire Qi can weaken the negative #3 star, which is of the Wood element. Have this red colour at the South West corner of the kitchen. But do remember that 'colour' is not very strong in terms of Qi quality. Especially when you only have four small accents of red – I would think a red lamp or light bulb would be a better representation of Fire Qi.

No Luo Pan, Can Do Feng Shui

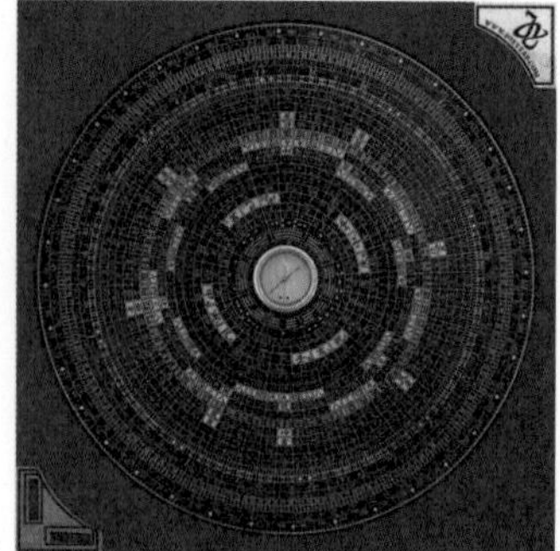

Recently, I read a book which stated that Feng Shui is divided into Form School and Compass School. Based on this classification, is it safe to assume that Form School does not need a compass for analysis?

It is a widespread fallacy that Feng Shui is divided into Form School and Compass School. There is no such thing as a 'Compass' school. All systems of Feng Shui advocate the use of a compass and this includes what is commonly referred to as 'Form School'.

You can say that Feng Shui is divided into Forms and Li Qi (Qi) Schools of thought. Forms refer to environmental factors whereas Li Qi refer to theories and calculations relating to Qi in an environment. Directions and Time factors are an integral part of all systems of Feng Shui. So a compass for directional analysis is an indispensable tool for any Feng Shui practitioner. If you get a practitioner who comes to your house empty-handed, you should be seriously suspicious!

If It Moves, Feng Shui It!

The proliferation of English language books on the subject of Feng Shui has rather, unfortunately, given rise to this notion that any object, big or small, has a Feng Shui significance. This is not the case! Still, I do get a lot of mail inquiring about the Feng Shui significance of all kinds of things! Flowers in particular, seem to have acquired a bit of a bad reputation!

Recently, I had a car accident while driving to work. I suffered a whiplash and my back still hurts. My wife thinks that the Feng Shui of my car is bad. Is there anything you can advise to help me improve my car's Feng Shui? Or should I sell the car?

Interesting question. I think you might have gotten the wrong idea about Feng Shui and its application. Feng Shui has nothing to do with your vehicle as it deals with matters relating to the environment, your house/building, you as the resident and time. (Unless you sleep in your car...)

Your vehicle is not 'Feng Shui-able' because it is firstly not a landed property, and it does not have a fixed location or direction. Direction and Location factors are very important aspects of Feng Shui formula calculations.

However, if you are looking for a 'protection amulet' or something to that effect, the best person to ask would be a spiritual master. A Feng Shui practitioner is not always a spiritual master, the two studies are very different.

Of course, this is not to say that your car accident is entirely without any relevance to Feng Shui but it has nothing to do with your car, more to do with your house.

Do pigeons carry good news to a home? My friend says that this is good Feng Shui to have pigeons flying into my yard, which is supposed to mean good news from afar.

There is nothing in Classical Feng Shui principles that states that 'pigeons' will bring good tidings. Feng Shui is mainly a study of directional and locational Qi factors of a property. Birds or other aerial animals are not part of the factors that influence the calculation of a house chart. It might be logical to assume that animals are more sensitive to pleasant Qi. Perhaps this is why they might land in your house and not on your neighbours. But, if this principle was true, then you should not only attract pigeons, but other types of birds too!

My boyfriend gave me a bouquet of dried roses. They are really beautiful and I've placed them next to my bed. My friend tells me it is bad to have dead flowers in the house, that they are bad Feng Shui and that my boyfriend wants to dump me for another woman. Is this true? Please help.

If dead flowers are bad, then all your furniture in your house needs to be thrown out of your house too because it is made of dead wood! I don't think anyone sensible would do this. You should ask your friend if she would throw her tables and chairs out because they are, in her own words 'bad Feng Shui'. So don't worry.

Feng Shui unfortunately has been mired with superstition. Many people cannot tell the difference between genuine Feng Shui and the 'superstitious' housewife beliefs. Dried flowers are fine and they are not bad Feng Shui in any way!

My husband bought me a very beautiful bouquet of dried flowers. I read that this is bad Feng Shui - dried flowers symbolise bad romance. But if I throw them away, it seems a little ungrateful to my husband. Is there anything I can do to counteract the bad Feng Shui?

Dried flowers are not bad Feng Shui. Who told you that? There's nothing wrong with dried flowers. Remember, flowers are a wonderful gesture of love from your husband, dried, fresh, pickled or preserved! By all means, keep them and display them prominently.

I'm totally new to Feng Shui. Recently, a friend of mine who "knows" a lot about Feng Shui told me that I have a huge problem. She said my bedroom is a marriage disaster zone because I have a King-sized bed. She told me I need to get rid of it or my marriage will be destined to end at anytime. I would like to know, how can a bed affect a marriage? And second, is there anything I can do to "cure" my bed? If I need to buy a new bed, what kind should I buy?

What has the size of your bed got to do with the marriage? Yes, it is the matrimonial bed BUT there are millions of people who sleep in King-sized beds and are STILL enjoying a good marriage. Equally, there are those who are having rotten marriages sleeping in Queen-sized beds.

Let's however give your friend the benefit of the doubt - perhaps she was referring to the ROOM or the POSITION in which you placed your bed. If your position or the room is not good, just change rooms or move your bed. You don't have to throw your bed away.

The next time you get marital advice from your friend of the Feng Shui kind, do yourself (and your marriage) a favour: JUST ASK WHY.

I read somewhere that in order to conceive successfully, I need to put symbols and pictures that represent fertility and children in my West wall. I was also told to find a small boy who is born in the year of the Dragon to roll over my bed and invoke his Yang Qi to help me conceive. Is this for real?

Frankly, I have never heard of this practice of asking a small boy to roll over a bed to invoke Yang Qi. There are other simpler ways of conceiving using Classical Feng Shui and you need not do any rituals or hang any pictures or find a suitably born little boy!

First, find out what your Gua number is. Next, make use of the Yan Nian direction (you can ascertain this by using the 8 Mansions calculator at www.masteryacademy.com). What do I mean by making use of the direction? There are several ways to do this: sleep in the Yan Nian room or direction or have your stove's fire mouth pointed to your Yan Nian direction.

Fear Factor

While Feng Shui attracts a lot of interest because of its perceived ability to make wealth, it also tends to create a lot of needless fear and paranoia.

I have open shelves facing me in my study room. I heard this is 'cutting Qi' and will hurt me. What can I do to negate this effect?

Open shelves are not a source of Cutting Qi or Sha Qi. The same goes for vertical blinds and edges of plaster ceilings. In Feng Shui we must always remember to first look at the bigger perspective. Small things like these often cause much paranoia but they really do not have any ill effects.

If there was a beam right above you or a distinct corner of the wall pointing directly at you, then okay, you might be hit by Sha-Qi. But shelves? No, they are fine as they are and where they are!

I have heard from a friend of mine that a house with the land sloping down at the back is not very favourable. Is this true?

Firstly, not all pieces of land where the rear slopes backwards are viewed as unfavourable in Feng Shui. This is only a general principle. On the contrary, certain properties are better if the backyard slopes down while other properties may be better if the front is lower than the back.

If you really want to know if a rear sloping land is favourable or unfavourable, plot the house's Flying Star chart. Superimpose the chart over your house plan and determine if you have the 'Prosperous Facing Stars' at the back of the home. Facing Stars like #8, #9 and #1 at the rear of your property coupled with land that is sloping backwards is fine.

Our neighbour across the road from us has a Ba Gua on his garage doors facing us. Is there anything we can do to place mirror or something on our house or is this okay? It faces into our son's bedroom window and our bedroom window as well. Is it okay?

You can safely ignore it. What makes you think a Ba Gua mirror has got any mystical powers that can direct evil Qi at you?

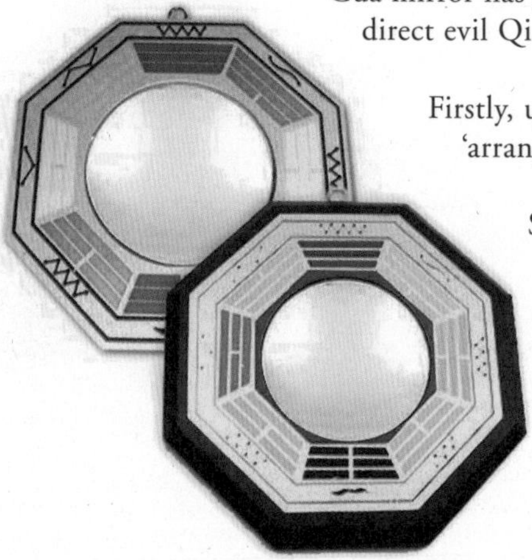

Firstly, understand that a Ba Gua is mainly an 'arrangement' of trigram lines.

Secondly, a BaGua is just another form of mirror. Don't let some of the descriptions in the Internet scare you. You see, in the old days, mirrors were made of bronze or copper simply because they lacked the technology to make mirrors. Later on, Feng Shui practitioners began using these as Metal cures to weaken negative stars like #5 and #2.

How it came to be made in the form of a Ba Gua can perhaps be traced back to spiritual reasons rather than Feng Shui. A mirror itself, be it a Ba Gua or not, cannot harm your home or family. All it does is reflect light. If you feel very uncomfortable with the idea psychologically, then just keep the curtains facing that window closed or install a venetian blind!

Toilet Humour

I get a lot of questions about toilets. People always want to know whether toilets are bad, where should they put their toilets, what colour the toilet (or toilet door) should be... the truth is, toilets are not really that important (in Feng Shui at least!).

Can you please tell me if it is true that I must always keep the toilet lid closed to avoid bad Qi from coming out to infest my house? Or is it true that the toilet sucks and flushes Qi away?

In the old days, the toilet system was not very hygienic. The smell was also bad for the very same reason. So naturally, bad Qi would be emitted from any unclosed toilets. However, today, toilets are much cleaner and much more hygienic. So even if you don't close your toilet lid, it doesn't matter.

Sometimes we need to focus on the bigger picture like the location of the rooms rather than what colors to paint on which wall and whether or not to close a toilet lid. If you think about it, there are many 'holes' in the water basins in our kitchens and toilets. But we don't plug these holes every time they are not used, right?

Feng Shui is not about worrying over the many, many small factors that do not have a serious impact.

Is it true that having a toilet in your good sector or auspicious area means you are flushing your luck down the toilet? Someone told me that toilets should always be located in your negative sectors.

Let me assure you that toilets do not 'flush' the luck away, whether located in good sectors or bad sectors. They're just toilets – plain and

simple. Imagine what trouble a house owner would have if they have a double story house and they have to put all the toilets only in the bad sectors. It's plain inconvenient and frankly silly to think toilets have such a powerful impact.

Instead of worrying about where your toilet is located (and whether the 'throne' has to face your favourable direction – the answer is no), focus instead on making sure that your Main Door opens in a good direction (if you practice Eight Mansions Feng Shui) or opens where a Prosperous Star is located (go for the #8 or #9 for Period 8 if you practice Flying Star Feng Shui). Make sure your Kitchen Stove and Master Bedroom are located in good sectors or areas with good stars. (and trust me, the toilets will take care of themselves!).

I read somewhere that toilets are Negative Qi – but what does this mean? I can't avoid going to the toilet!

Toilets are by and large neutral when it comes to Feng Shui. Unless of course it is extremely unhygenic. In Feng Shui, we are mainly concerned with areas of the residence which are actively used or frequented by the residents. Why for example is so much prominence placed on the Main Door, the Kitchen Stove and the Master Bedroom? (and in recent years, the study)? Because these are places that we either always use (how else do you come into the house but through the Main Door?), spend a lot of time in (8 hours a day are spent sleeping so the bedroom is an important place) or cook the food that we eat.

Hence, it is important that the Qi in these areas is prosperous and auspicious, and they provide a harmonious and good environment for us to sleep, work and live in.

Unless you happen to also live in your toilet and sleep there, it doesn't really matter too much where it is located (other than being in a convenient location). Even if, for the sake of argument, toilets do have Negative Qi, given the few minutes most of us spend in them, it's really not enough to have much impact.

A Question of Qi

Qi unfortunately has become a bit of an over-used word. It is one of those words, like zen, that has entered into the public vocabulary and has become so common that no one really knows what it means any more. So much so, Qi is now appended to everything, from cups and mugs to crystals and what have you!

This is the first time I am writing in and I would appreciate it very much if you could answer my question. Is it necessary to use bright lights to brighten up every dark area of my house? My wife says the books say this helps loosen up stuck Qi and make good Feng Shui?

There is no need to brighten up every corner of your house with lamps. I think this would be a sheer waste of electricity rather than serving to improve the Feng Shui.

Good Qi (or Bad Qi) very much depends on the environmental features and internal features of your house. If your house's Main Door opens to allow good Qi to come in, then your house already enjoys good Qi. But if your house receives bad Qi, then no matter how many lamps you have and no matter how much brightening you do, you're not going to improve the situation.

A plant in my living room which I placed to block the straight path of Sha Qi from my staircase to the main door keeps drying up and dying. I have to change the plant every few months. Is this because of the Bad Qi that rushes out from my staircase?

Hmm – perhaps you do not have enough sunlight or good soil for the potted plant? A client of mine experienced the same problem; his leafy plant kept dying on him. Later I found out that it was not getting enough sunlight simply because no one remembered to take it for a 'walk' outdoors. Remember, sometimes the situation has nothing to do with Feng Shui but everything to do with basic gardening!

I've heard a lot about how a lamp post is considered 'negative' in Feng Shui. Can you please elaborate what a lamp post can or cannot do to the Qi of the house. Street light lamp posts either give out yellow or white light. Do different light colors affect the Qi of the house in different ways?

The answer to your first question is, it doesn't matter what color of light the lamp post emits, what matters more is where its location is in relation to the house. Especially here in Malaysia, some lamp posts have the electrical wires badly exposed and this can be regarded as a 'negative' environmental trait. Depending on its location and proximity to your Main Door, it can negatively affect the stars in that sector.

Wood Wife Metal Husband = Doom?

I've been teaching and practicing BaZi for a couple of years and sometimes, people who have heard about BaZi and know a little Feng Shui tend to get confused between the two.

Is it true that the Earth people cannot have furniture made of wood in the house? I love teak furniture but my Self Element is Earth.

It is totally untrue that Earth people cannot have Wood furniture. This is simply absurd, like saying Fire people should not drink Water. It's funny what many people can come up with these days - don't worry.

I am the element of Wood according to my BaZi. But my Ming Gua is of the Metal element. Which one should I follow?

For Feng Shui purposes you should follow your Ming Gua (or Life Gua). For Chinese Astrology and Destiny Analysis, you should follow your Self Element in your BaZi.

Contrary to popular misconception, the Ming Gua's element is NOT for 'enhancing'. This is a popular but misguided assumption by students initially starting out in their study of Feng Shui. If for example you are Gua #9 (Li or Fire) that does not mean you need to paint your room red to enhance your Ming Gua. From this you can see that Ming Gua is not supposed to be applied in this manner.

Your Ming Gua is used as a reference to your personal Qi in the Feng Shui of your home. If you are serious in using elements or colours to help yourself, refer to your BaZi Element. Find out what your Favourable Element is and then undertake to wear colours that will help you. But remember, colours at most only have about plus or minus 10 percent impact. When it comes to BaZi, taking the right action is much more important.

I recently discovered that my husband and I are in different Gua groups (he is East, I am West). How on earth are we going to coordinate our auspicious directions? What about our bedroom? Should we sleep in separate beds? (it's a romance killer but...)

My first piece of advice is don't panic. It is NOT the case in Feng Shui (specifically Eight Mansions Feng Shui) that East is East and West is West and never the twain shall meet! You and your husband can continue to sleep in the same room, and you can sleep in the same bed.

It is patently ridiculous that merely because you and your husband are not of the same Direction group, you should have separate bedrooms, separate studies – should this extend to separate kitchens as well? Remember that the Life Gua is just one factor in Eight Mansions Feng Shui and not a very significant factor for that matter. The House Gua is much more important – so it's more important to make sure that your bedroom is located in a GOOD SECTOR of the House according to the House Gua so both of you can enjoy good Qi at the same time.

I am in a bit of a crisis. I met a really nice guy recently and we seemed to get along quite well. However, when I checked his BaZi, I found that he's Metal and I'm Wood. Does this mean I will be 'chopped' by him? Does this mean I should rule him out as a prospective husband?

Compatibility analysis is a rather sophisticated and complex analysis skill in BaZi and cannot be based on just the Day Master or Self Element. This would mean that Wood people cannot marry Metal people, Fire people cannot marry Water people and so forth! Certainly not true.

Aquarium Angst

After the fish, comes the aquarium. But unlike the fish, which has a rather frivolous superstitious reputation following around it, the aquarium is an important matter. It is important to place it in the right place (but don't stress about the fish please...)

My kids have a pair of small pet turtles we bought some months back. We keep them (turtles, not our kids) in a plastic container half filled with water in the NE sector of my home (Period 7, West 2 facing, Main Door facing West 2) which also happens to be where the back door is. Will the presence of water here affect us in any way? I'm concerned about my husband's work as his study is upstairs in the North East sector also. I removed my aquarium from the South East this year due to the 5 Yellow and hence do not have any water features in my home. My North West sector which has the Water Star 8 is a missing sector (drat!). Would really appreciate your comments. Thanks.

A small little plastic container is not going to affect you much, so don't worry about it. Otherwise you might end up being too busy worrying about where you place your glass of water and cup of coffee around your house! In 2004 you can reposition your aquarium in the South East sector.

Even though the West is the most auspicious corner for the year 2003 it is also "Three Killings" star corner. Can I put my aquarium here since I have had it here for more than 3 years already or do I need to remove it to other places of my house? My house main entrance is at the West.

Your aquarium does not affect the Three Killings in any way. 3 Killings are only activated when you start digging the ground in the West of your home. An aquarium will not disturb this Sha Qi. A small aquarium may even help you with the activation of the #8 wealth star, located in the West this year.

However there may be some small side effects as this is also the Direct Spirit sector for Period 7. The corresponding drawback, if any, will depend on what original stars you have in your West palace as well as your individual Gua and Life Palace.

One of my bedrooms is occupied by water (Facing) Star #8. Can I put my aquarium there? I heard that it will bring bad luck by putting an aquarium in the bedroom but the thing is, we never sleep in this room since it is a spare room. Your advice is most appreciated as this corner is the most auspicious corner in my house that I can activate.

Of course you can put Water there to activate the #8 Facing Star. But you must first determine if this sector is suitable for water. As a guide, if this Facing Star #8 is residing in the North, then it is okay to use water. If unsure, then just put a small water feature to test out its effects. If you see improvements, then enlarge the size of your water feature.

However, it might be better if you can use this room as a workroom. The more business activities you do in a Facing Star #8 room, the more beneficial because you are directly influenced by its Qi. Keeping it as a guest room is a waste of all the good Wealth Qi!

True Stories: Feng Shui In Practice

Sometimes I get very specific questions in my mailbag. I try my best to offer guidance and advice to those who have sought my assistance. Some of the advice is quite technical in nature, but you'll find most of it becomes clear once you have some knowledge of Flying Star Feng Shui, Xuan Kong or Eight Mansions (Ba Zhai) Feng Shui.

My house directions: Facing North West, main door facing North West 2/3 and Period 7 house. According to my house's Flying Star chart, the Water (Facing) Star #8 is trapped smack in the center of my house which happens to be a corridor connecting the front door to the back of the house, hence two facing wall (ie. South West and North East side).

Upon doing the small Tai Ji of the area, the possibility of placing a water feature (to activate the Water Star #8) is along the North East wall which has a Mountain Star #9, and South West wall which has the unlucky Mountain Star #3. My friend says to place the water feature at a corner but which corner? Don't want to activate # 9 Mountain Star. Can't place in the middle either as it is a corridor. Can you suggest another suitable water spot feature for the remaining months of 2003? I would really like to improve my financial situation/career.

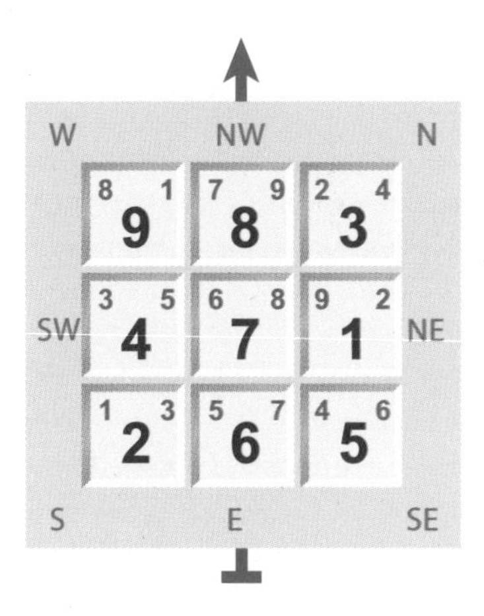

The idea is to get the #8 Facing Star out of its present 'trapped' position. There are traditional and modern techniques. Your friend may have suggested the modern (and safer) approach. It doesn't matter against which wall, the idea is, it should be where the #8 is, to activate it accordingly. Do try your best to allow the front palace to reach the center of your home so Qi can flow freely. If your center is tight and narrow, then this #8 is trapped and the water can't help much.

The alternative is the Facing Star #9 location. This is the secondary wealth position you can try to tap into. It is not always necessary to use 'water' to activate the stars. The right allocation of the door and pathways can be just as effective.

I intend to buy an under-construction house this week and the house is scheduled to be completed with CFO towards the end of next year. My problem now is that I am trying to choose a house suited to my family's direction and I hope you can help. The house that we intend to buy is facing North East (NE).

I understand that we are from the West group, so our preferable directions are of West, North East, North West and South West. I understand too that beginning from year 2004, we will be in the Period 8 which will last for another 20 years but does that mean that the directions for the West group will change? If so, which are the directions for the West group people then? If no, is it advisable to get the house with the mentioned positioning?

The house has a sliding door that opens from the right side and when it is opened, it faces the toilet in the house directly. I intend to change the opening of the sliding door (if I were to buy later) and have it opened in the middle to avoid the toilet. I heard from some people that it is a bad idea to have a door opened from the middle – I would appreciate your guidance on this also.

I urgently need your advice because I am given 2 days by the developer to decide. If not, the unit will be opened to other interested buyers.

Let me try to answer your questions section by section, so it's clear.

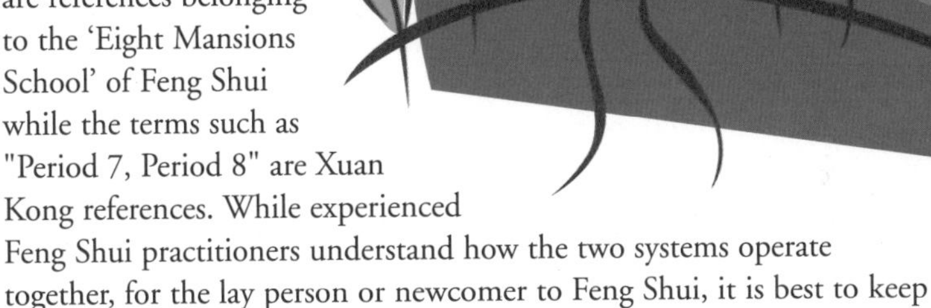

First question: Does the direction of West/East people change in Period 8? The direction of West group people will NOT change. West Group and East Group are references belonging to the 'Eight Mansions School' of Feng Shui while the terms such as "Period 7, Period 8" are Xuan Kong references. While experienced Feng Shui practitioners understand how the two systems operate together, for the lay person or newcomer to Feng Shui, it is best to keep them both separate so as to avoid needless confusion and concern.

Second question: The best direction for your family. It would be ideal for you and your family of course to find a property that faces NE. Generally, this would be better. However if you do choose to purchase this North Facing house, then you might need to adjust the door to tap the North East Qi. If you can do this, you will also avoid the direct alignment with the toilet as you've described.

House and door direction TZU - 356 degrees. The house was built in 1971 (we do not know what month) The house is on a cul-de-sac and it is 2 doors away from the center house at the end of the cul-de-sac which puts it within the circle at the end. Just under 26 feet from the door is a large tree. (It is a beautiful river birch about 20 years old and I trim it so its branches do not hit the front part of the roof. We love it but understand that it may be a problem - we hope not.)

We have done some major remodeling - turned the major part of the garage into a dining room, put in a raised floor so it would be

at the same level as the rest of the house; created a new entrance from the living room into the new dining room. Put a wall up between what used to be the dining room and the kitchen - it was one big continuous space and now we have an office/Reiki room.

We did not change the roof line of the house, we simply made the garage a living space. So has the period of our home changed from 6 to 7 or is it still Period 6? It is important for me to know this so I can plot out my star chart.

We have lived in this home since 1987 and though I feel it is problematic for both my husband and I (we are always struggling financially) our sons have done quite well. We can't complain really because we have managed to send both our boys to very good schools that we couldn't really afford from the time they were 13 and yet somehow we have been able to do it.

We are happily married for 28 years - we sleep in the NW with our heads pointing towards the West - but we are tired of only making ends meet no matter what we do. If this house is draining us, I would like to do something about it since we are not in a position to sell it and move at this time.

Your major remodeling of your home coupled with your new entrance would have made the home a Period 7 house and you would base your analysis on a Period 7 Natal chart.

To read a flying star chart, we need to understand the positions of your main door, or entrances into your home, what sort of Qi comes in and out of these entrances and of course, how the external environment outside every sector affects /activates /deactivates the stars.

Good stars alone may not exert any good effects without the right external conditions and the right 'people' using these stars.

To focus and improve your financial goals, I would advise you to seek out the #8 and #9 Facing stars of your property. Activate them with water if the sector permits. Some sectors are not conducive for water placements so you might want to be careful with this.

In 2004, the wealth positions are in North East and South. Use these sectors as frequently as possible in order to benefit from the Qi in the area. Also, do keep an eye out for the monthly afflictions and influences as these are also crucial factors in maximizing the positive Qi in your home.

I would like to seek your advice with regards to changing my house to a Period 8 property. My Gua Number is 6 and my wife is 3. My house has a SE1 facing direction. I used to have a door (now a window) at the South cum SE location (facing SE) but as I am a West group person, I was advised a few years ago and I subsequently installed a door facing NE, facing the garage (located in the SE).

With Period 8 coming, I understand that it would be best to have my main door facing SE2/3 to tap the Water Star 8. The Mountain Star 8 will then be at the back of my house, which will be good as my back neighbor's house is on higher ground.

If I install a new main door at the South cum SE location and align it to be facing SE2/3, do I need to do anything with my old door i.e. realign, take out?

Also, I was told by a Feng Shui practitioner to align the new front door at 135 degrees for best effect. Is there a reason for this? Wouldn't it be adequate as long as it's between 127.5 - 157.5 degrees?

As a West group person, should I continue to use the old door to exit and enter on a daily basis or should I use the new main door?

Your plan to renew the house for Period 8 is correct. Your main door however should be in the SE sector and not the South sector. The #8 facing star is in the SE sector of your SE2/3 Period 8 home.

I think you might have misunderstood the degrees or got it wrong. 135 degrees is a 'death and emptiness' line. I think it should be 137 degrees. I believe the reason was that your Feng Shui practitioner might be using Xuan Kong Da Gua but I cannot confirm this without knowing if he or she has advised you on special locations for secondary doors, water and mountain positions in certain specific degrees in your house.

A good practitioner must know WHEN to forgo the East/West group principle in favor of some other more beneficial formations in Feng Shui. Based on the information you've given me, I would suggest you to use your SE door, even though it is not one of your favorable directions. A person's individual direction is not the most important thing in Feng Shui. It is only a very elementary consideration and its effects are not as strong as other important factors such as location Qi. So, use the new main door.

I got a very famous Feng Shui master to do my house. I have studied some Flying Stars and asked him questions. But he scolded me and told me Flying Stars is rubbish and I must follow my Ba Zhai (8 Mansions Feng Shui) direction.

He asked me to put my cooker in the North West and asked me to shift my door to the South East. He also told me to sleep facing South East in my room. I thought this was weird because my bed then faces a corner of the room.

After I did the change, my situation went from good to jobless. I tried to call him but he is always not in. Then when I finally reached him he scolded me again and told me it's my karma. And he insisted that it is already my best direction and if it doesn't work is because I don't have a good karma.

My house now faces South and it looks ugly to have a door slanted to the southeast at an ugly angle. Should I change my door by tilting?

Door tilting should always be a last resort. As much as possible, we'd like to try and avoid door tilts as it resembles a crooked Qi mouth. Which means Qi will be difficult to flow into your house.

Whether or not it is your best direction (since I don't know your Gua), any door tilt must be made in consideration of the environmental features. In your case, you have also accidentally activated the #5 Yellow in the South East last year 2003.

I don't agree that Flying Star Feng Shui is rubbish and that Ba Zhai is more important or takes precedence over this.

Both systems are important but the application of a particular system over another depends on the situation.

Your house faces the South direction and this is the 3 Killings for 2004. If you plan to make any changes, you'll need to ensure you have selected a suitable date, based on your exact house direction and your personal BaZi.

About Joey Yap

Joey Yap is the founder and Master Trainer of the Mastery Academy of Chinese Metaphysics, a global organisation devoted to the worldwide teaching of Feng Shui, BaZi, Mian Xiang and other Chinese Metaphysics subjects. Joey is also the CEO of Yap Global Consulting, a Feng Shui and Chinese Astrology consulting firm offering audit and consultation services to corporations and individuals all over the world.

Joey received his formal education in Malaysia and Australia. He has combined the best of Eastern learning and Western education systems in the teaching methodology practiced at the Academy. Students of the Mastery Academy study traditional syllabuses of Chinese Metaphysics but through Western-style modular programs that are structured and systematic, enabling individuals to easily and quickly learn, grasp and master complex Chinese Metaphysics subjects like Feng Shui and BaZi. These unique structured learning systems are also utilized by Mastery Academy instructors all over the world to teach BaZi and Feng Shui.

The Mastery Academy is also the first international educational organisation to fully utilize the benefits of the Internet to promote continuous education, encourage peer-to-peer learning, enable mentoring and distance learning. Students interact with each other 'live', and continue to learn and improve their knowledge.

Despite his busy schedule, Joey continues to write for the Mastery Journal, a monthly eZine on Feng Shui and Astrology and the production of the world's first bilingual Ten Thousand Year Calendar. He is also the author of two forthcoming books, an anthology of stories on Feng Shui and a book on BaZi or Four Pillars.

Author's personal website: www.joeyyap.com
Academy website: www.masteryacademy.com

EDUCATION

The Mastery Academy of Chinese Metaphysics: the first choice for practitioners and aspiring students of the art and science of Chinese Classical Feng Shui and Astrology.

For thousands of years, Eastern knowledge has been passed from one generation to another through the system of discipleship. A venerated Master would accept suitable individuals at a young age as his disciples, and informally through the years, pass on his knowledge and skills to them. His disciples in turn, would take on their own disciples, as a means to perpetuate knowledge or skills.

This system served the purpose of restricting the transfer of knowledge to only worthy honourable individuals and ensuring that outsiders or Westerners would not have access to thousands of years of Eastern knowledge, learning and research.
However, the disciple system has also resulted in Chinese Metaphysics and Classical Studies lacking systematic teaching methods. Knowledge garnered over the years has not been accumulated in a concise, systematic manner, but scattered amongst practitioners, each practicing his/her knowledge, art and science, in isolation.

The disciple system, out of place in today's modern world, endangers the advancement of these classical fields that continue to have great relevance and application today.

At the Mastery Academy of Chinese Metaphysics, our Mission is to bring Eastern Classical knowledge in the fields of Metaphysics, Feng Shui and Astrology sciences and the arts to the world. These Classical teachings and knowledge, previously shrouded in secrecy and passed on only through the discipleship system, are adapted into structured learning, which can easily be understood, learnt and mastered. Through modern learning methods, these renowned ancient arts, sciences and practices can be perpetuated while facilitating more extensive application and understanding of these classical subjects.

The Mastery Academy espouses an educational philosophy that draws from the best of the East and West . It is the world's premier educational institution for the studies of Chinese Metaphysics, offering a wide range and variety of courses, ensuring that students have the opportunity to pursue their preferred field of study and enabling existing practitioners and professionals to gain cross-disciplinary knowledge that complements their current field of practice.

Courses at the Mastery Academy have been carefully designed to ensure a comprehensive yet compact syllabus. The modular nature of the courses enables students to immediately begin to put their knowledge into practice while pursuing continued study of their field and complementary fields. Students thus have the benefit of developing and gaining practical experience in tandem with the expansion and advancement of their theoretical knowledge.

Students can also choose from a variety of study options, from a distance learning program, the Homestudy Series, that enables study at one's own pace or intensive foundation courses and compact lecture-based courses, held in various cities around the world by Joey Yap or our licensed instructors. The Mastery Academy's faculty and make-up is international in nature, thus ensuring that prospective students can attend courses at destinations nearest to their country of origin or with a licensed Mastery Academy instructor in their home country.

The Mastery Academy provides 24x7 support to students through its Online Community, with a variety of tools, documents, forums and e-learning materials to help students stay at the forefront of research in their fields and gain invaluable assistance from peers and mentoring from their instructors.

19-3, The Boulevard, Mid Valley City,
Lingkaran Syed Putra,
59200 Kuala Lumpur, Malaysia.
Tel: +603-2284 8080, +603-2284 8318
Fax: +603-2284 1218
Email: info@masteryacademy.com
Website: www.masteryacademy.com

JOIN OUR FENG SHUI COMMUNITY

The Mastery Academy Community is a meeting place for students and enthusiasts of Feng Shui, Chinese Astrology and various other studies of Chinese Metaphysics to mingle and interact with one another. Here you can discuss your Feng Shui studies, ask a question and get it answered by a senior, instructor or even Joey Yap personally.

Accessing the Community is easy. It has a user-friendly interface, there is no software to download or install and you will be able to access the Community from anywhere in the world as long as you have an Internet connection. It's also free to access the Community.

Do take the opportunity to browse the archives on your first visit. You may find the answer to your question amongst the many postings to the community from various enthusiasts of Feng Shui from around the world.

To Join the Mastery Academy Community:

1. Go to www.masteryacademy.com

2. Click on the link on top that says COMMUNITY and once inside this page, click on the Registration link.

3. Fill up the information and click Register.

4. Your new Mastery Academy ID and Password will be mailed to your e-mail address.

5. Use this to login to the Mastery Academy Community.

Please do read the FAQ's and the Rules and Regulations of the Community. That section will provide you with an idea of what is permitted and how to best make use of the forums. Should you face any problems or need assistance at any time, please e-mail community@masteryacademy.com or call + 603-2284-8080.

Continue Your Journey with Joey Yap's Books

The Ten Thousand Year Calendar

The Ten Thousand Year Calendar or 萬年曆 Wan Nian Li is a regular reference book and an invaluable tool used by masters, practitioners and students of Feng Shui, BaZi (Four Pillars of Destiny), Chinese Zi Wei Dou Shu Astrology (Purple Star), Yi Jing (I-Ching) and Date Selection specialists.

JOEY YAP's Ten Thousand Year Calendar provides the Gregorian (Western) dates converted into both the Chinese Solar and Lunar calendar in both the English and Chinese language.

It also includes a comprehensive set of key Feng Shui and Chinese Astrology charts and references, including Xuan Kong Nine Palace Flying Star Charts, Monthly and Daily Flying Stars, Water Dragon Formulas Reference Charts, Zi Wei Dou Shu (Purple Star) Astrology Reference Charts, BaZi (Four Pillars of Destiny) Heavenly Stems, Earthly Branches and all other related reference tables for Chinese Metaphysical Studies

Stories and Lessons on Feng Shui

Stories and Lessons on Feng Shui is a compilation of essays and stories written by leading Feng Shui and Chinese Astrology trainer and consultant Joey Yap about Feng Shui and Chinese Astrology.

In this heart-warming collection of easy to read stories, find out why it's a myth that you should never have Water on the right hand side of your house, the truth behind the infamous 'love' and 'wealth' corners and that the sudden death of a pet fish is really NOT due to bad luck!

Elevate Your Feng Shui Skills With Joey Yap's Home Study Course And Educational DVDs

---

Xuan Kong Vol.1

An Advanced Feng Shui Home Study Course

Learn the Xuan Kong Flying Star Feng Shui system in just 20 lessons! Joey Yap's specialised notes and course work have been written to enable distance learning without compromising on the breadth or quality of the syllabus. Learn at your own pace and learn the same material students in a live class would learn. The most comprehensive distance learning course on Xuan Kong Flying Star Feng Shui in the market. Xuan Kong Flying Star Vol 1 comes complete with a special binder for all your course notes.

Xuan Kong 10-Day Video Coaching Program

In 10 days and just 10 lessons, learn step-by-step from Joey Yap himself the fundamentals of Xuan Kong Flying Star Feng Shui. Comes complete with a Journal for students to record important notes and reference key diagrams and charts. It's like being in class with Joey, in the comfort of your own living room.

Feng Shui for Period 8 - (DVD)

Don't miss the Feng Shui Event of the next 20 years! Catch Joey Yap LIVE and find out just what Period 8 is all about. This DVD boxed set zips you through the fundamentals of Feng Shui and the impact of this important change in the Feng Shui calendar. Joey's entertaining, conversational style walks you through the key changes that Period 8 will bring and how to tap into Wealth Qi and Good Feng Shui for the next 20 years.

Xuan Kong Flying Stars Beginners Workshop - DVD

Take a front row seat in Joey Yap's Xuan Kong Flying Stars workshop with this unique LIVE RECORDING of Joey Yap's Xuan Kong Flying Stars Feng Shui workshop, attended by over 500 people. This DVD program is an effective and quick introduction of Xuan Kong Feng Shui essentials for those who are just starting out in their study of classical Feng Shui. Learn to plot your own Flying Star chart in just 3 hours. Learn 'trade secret' methods, remedies and cures for Flying Stars Feng Shui. This boxed set contains 3 DVDs and 1 workbook with notes and charts for reference.

BaZi Four Pillars of Destiny Beginners Workshop - (DVD)

Ever wondered what Destiny has in store for you? Or curious to know how you can learn more about your personality and inner talents? BaZi or Four Pillars of Destiny is an ancient Chinese science that enables us to understand a person's hidden talent, inner potential, personality, health and wealth luck from just their birth data. This specially compiled DVD set of Joey Yap's BaZi Beginners Workshop provides a thorough and comprehensive introduction to BaZi. Learn how to read your own chart and understand your own luck cycle. This boxed set contains 3 DVDs, 1 workbook with notes and reference charts.

BaZi Mastery Series™

BaZi Mastery – Module 1
Intensive Foundation Course

This Intensive One Day Foundation Course provides an introduction to the principles and fundamentals of BaZi (Four Pillars of Destiny) and Destiny Analysis methods such as Ten Gods, Useful God and Strength of Qi. Learn how to plot a BaZi chart and interpret your Destiny and your potential. Master BaZi and learn to capitalize on your strengths, minimize risks and downturns and take charge of your Destiny.

BaZi Mastery – Module Two
Practical BaZi Applications

BaZi Module Two teaches students advanced BaZi analysis techniques and specific analysis methods for relationship luck, health evaluation, wealth potential and career potential. Students will learn to identify BaZi chart structures, sophisticated methods for applying the Ten Gods, and how to read Auxiliary Stars. Students who have completed Module Two will be able to conduct professional BaZi readings.

BaZi Mastery – Module Three
Advanced Practitioners Program

Designed for the BaZi practitioner, learn how to read complex cases and unique events in BaZi charts and perform Big and Small assessments. Discover how to analyze personalities and evaluate talents precisely, as well as special formulas and classical methodologies for BaZi from classics such as Di Tian Sui and Qiong Tong Bao Jian.

BaZi Mastery – Module Four
Master Course in BaZi

The graduating course of the BaZi Mastery Series, this course takes the advanced practitioner to the Masters' level. BaZi M4 focuses on specialized techniques of BaZi reading, unique special structures and advance methods from ancient classical texts. This program includes techniques on date selection and ancient methodologies from the Qiong Tong Bao Jian and Yuan Hai Zi Ping classics.

Xuan Kong Mastery Series™

Xuan Kong Mastery – Module One

Advanced Foundation Program

This course is for the experienced Feng Shui professionals who wish to expand their knowledge and skills in the Xuan Kong system of Feng Shui, covering important foundation methods and techniques from the Wu Chang and Guang Dong lineages of Xuan Kong Feng Shui.

Xuan Kong Mastery – Module 2A

Advanced Xuan Kong Methodologies

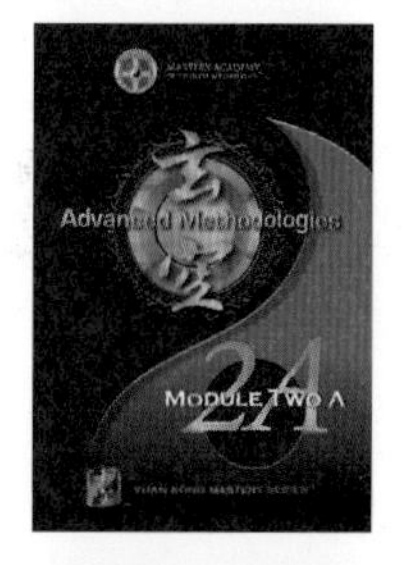

Designed for Feng Shui practitioners seeking to specialise in the Xuan Kong system, this program focuses on methods of application and Joey Yap's unique Life Palace and Shifting Palace Methods, as well as methods and techniques from the Wu Chang lineage.

Xuan Kong Mastery – Module 2B

Purple White

Explore in detail and in great depth the star combinations in Xuan Kong. Learn how each different combination reacts or responds in different palaces, under different environmental circumstances and to whom in the property. Learn methods, theories and techniques extracted from ancient classics such as Xuan Kong Mi Zhi, Xuan Kong Fu, Fei Xing Fu and Zi Bai Jue.

Xuan Kong Mastery – Module 3

Advanced Xuan Kong Da Gua

This intensive course focuses solely on the Xuan Kong Da Gua system covering the theories, techniques and methods of application of this unique 64-Hexagram based system of Xuan Kong including Xuan Kong Da Gua for landform analysis.